A STRAIGHTFORWARD GUIDE TO

THE RIGHTS OF DISABLED CHILDREN

Doreen Jarrett

Straightforward Guides

© Straightforward Publishing 2016

ISBN
978-1-84716-601-2

Printed by 4edge www.4edge.co.uk

Cover design by Bookworks Islington

CONTENTS

Ch.5 Education   63

Ch.6 Help With Transport and Equipment for You and   73
Your Disabled Child

Index

Appendix 1. An overview of welfare benefits

****

Introduction

Many parents of disabled children find the experience of looking after that child all the more difficult and traumatic because of the lack of information from the professionals who work in the field of disability. In addition to the initial trauma of finding that their child has been diagnosed as disabled, if a diagnosis has been made at all, parents can also be rendered powerless by a lack of information about their child's condition and the ongoing support that they need, plus knowledge of the services, support and benefits to which their child is entitled.

This book, it is hoped, will greatly assist the parent(s) of a disabled child and also help to empower and point them in the right direction, enabling people to obtain the support and advice that is needed, both in the early years and later in life.

This book doesn't give information on specific disabilities. This information can be obtained from various sources, such as MENCAP and local libraries, which have a lot of information concerning organisations that exist to provide advice and support. A particularly good organisation is Contact a Family www.cafamily.org.uk which exists to help parents with disabled children and has a wealth of information.

The book is aimed primarily at parent(s) but may be of interest to others such as professionals and agencies, and takes a very practical approach, dealing initially with a discussion of the early days, or months, after having a child diagnosed as disabled. The law and disability is then outlined, along with the professionals involved in the field of disability, and what they do and also the benefit system. Education is discussed, access to education and the responsibilities of local authorities. Holidays and breaks for disabled children and their parents are covered along with transport generally.

This book is a companion volume to A Straightforward Guide To The Rights of Disabled People, which covers the rights of adults who are disabled, either from birth or through accident. I hope it helps a great deal in your journey and makes life easier for both parent and child.

The book opens with a discussion of initial reactions and emotions of parents on learning that their child has a disability. This is a very important time and helps to set the book in context.

Doreen Jarrett

****

Chapter 1

The Early Days

When you have a child with a disability, you will have to cope with a number of issues. On one hand you will have to find your way through the maze of organisations that exist to help you as well as coping with your own emotions and the reactions of relatives and friends plus the reactions of siblings.

Some parents are given the news that their child has a disability at birth, or even before birth. Others might receive the diagnosis after months or years have elapsed. This very much depends on the particular condition. Depending on when you learn of a child's disability, your feelings will vary in reaction and also in intensity. These emotions will cover a whole range of feelings such as anger and disbelief, denial, frustration and guilt. Blame can be placed on oneself or one's partner, which is natural and should eventually pass as it can be rationalised over time. A certain amount of grief will be felt as, although you haven't lost the child you did not have the child that you expected. Ultimately, you will need to change the expectations that you had for him or her. Finally though, comes acceptance and the realisation that you need to live with the situation, love the child and give it the best that you can.

Depression is a common emotion, and can express itself through feelings of pessimism and hopelessness and lead to other difficulties such as problems with eating and sleeping. If you think that you are suffering from depression and recognise the signs then you will need to see your GP, and also in turn health visitors or other agencies.

As mentioned, for some parent's the actual diagnosis of a child's condition cannot be made until after a few years because certain things don't become evident until time has elapsed. This at least gives a parent time to adjust to what might be needed although it in no way diminishes the initial feelings of shock and anger.

Negative feelings towards the child

One of the emotions that you may find particularly difficult to deal with is that of harbouring negative feelings towards your child. The child may look different to others, although this is not always the case. It may take a time to develop a bond and love the child properly. This is perfectly normal and nothing to be ashamed of.

You may also feel over-protective which is a perfectly normal reaction. It can become problematic, however, if being over-protective prevents the child from attaining his or her own independence.

If you have feelings of wanting to harm your child then you will need to seek help immediately. Again, help can be obtained from various sources, such as your GP, health visitor or from a range of agencies detailed at the back of this book. Organisations such as Familylives, CRY-SIS and the NSPCC are particularly useful as they have a lot of experience in this area.

Coping with emotions

With time, and a lot of support, the vast majority of parent's do cope with their situation. They also grow to love their child and get a lot of pleasure from him or her. In the early days (months-years) the best way to cope with feelings that will inevitably arise from the discovery that your child has a disability is to be as open as possible and discuss your feelings with your partner, relatives and friends and also sympathetic professionals. As time goes by you will develop relations with professionals, those who you feel the most empathy with.

There are numerous groups dealing with all sorts of disabilities and they have networks of people who have been through the experience and can share their own experiences with you. You won't feel alone and can learn an awful lot.

It is also very important indeed to attempt to continue as normal a life as possible, going out to see friends for example. Doing the things that you enjoy and providing continuity in your own life is very important indeed and can provide balance.

Reactions of others in your life

Finally, in addition to coping yourself, you need to take into account the feelings of your own partner, if you have a partner or spouse, and ensure that you speak very openly and try to get along together on the same wavelength. Bottling up feelings is very unhealthy and can lead to problems. Relationships between parent's is one of the most important factors in how a family adjusts to disability and how family life develops.

If your partner is male and he is the father of the child, it is highly likely that he will experience the disability in a more negative way, in the first instance. Generally speaking, a mother will bond with a child more quickly than the father may and the father could experience feelings of rejection towards the child. Taking this into account, it is important that both parent's are fully involved with the child and it's development right from the outset, sharing care, appointments with professionals and overall responsibility for development of the child.

Relatives can also exhibit differing emotions, such as guilt (for example, have they been indirectly responsible because of a genetic problem?). It might be that elder relatives, such as grandparents, have an old fashioned view of disability and may need updating with information about the child's condition.

Relatives might want to help in areas such as babysitting and doing housework, and this will involve them more and also take some of the pressure of you.

There is also the question of reactions of friends. Hopefully, your friends will react positively and want to help. It is important, once again, to be as open as possible. Allow them to see the baby as soon as possible which will reinforce the fact that the baby is a person rather than a disability. Friends can also offer practical support, particularly if they are good friends and are intelligent and sympathetic.

Reactions of siblings

If you have children, it is important to tell them about the child's disability as soon as possible. This goes without saying. How much you tell your children will depend on how old they are. Generally, children under a certain age, say 3 years old, are still too young to understand details about the disability or condition of their sibling. They can, however, be told that you are feeling sad and that their new baby sister or brother needs a lot of care and attention.

Older children can be told a little more about their sibling's disability. Use simple terms and try not to confuse them. Most children, older children, will understand. It is important to remember that you will still need to divide your time equally between children so as not to exclude them. Above all, try to involve sibling's in the child's development.

Coping with disability, and the reactions to disability, and the attendant emotions, is not easy. However, very importantly, try to remember that you are not alone and that there are numerous support groups out there with a network of people who are only to willing to offer support and share their experiences.

In the next chapter, we will look at how the law impacts on disability. Although this is a dry area, it is important to understand as it will give you an idea of your rights and the child's rights.

****

Useful Contacts

KIDS is a leading disabled children's charity that has been in existence for over 40 years working to enable disabled children and young people and their families www.kids.org.uk

Disability Rights UK
Ground Floor
CAN Mezzanine
49-51 East Rd
London
N1 6AH
Tel:: 020 7250 8181
(this line open Mon-Fri, between 10.00 and 12.30pm and 1.30 and 4.00pm)

Child Disability help
Child-disability.co.uk
Organisation providing advice and support for parents of disabled children.

Contact a family
209-211 City Road
London EC1V 1JN
0208 7608 8700
Helpline 0808 808 3555
email helpline@cafamily.org.uk

MENCAP
123 Golden Lane
London
EC1Y ORT
020 7454 0454

Familylives

www.familylives.org.uk

0808 8002222

CRY-SIS

www.cry-sis.org.uk

08451 228 669

****

Chapter 2

The Law and Disability

Although this book is specifically about the rights of disabled children, those rights sit within the wider body of law that covers all people with disabilities. Below is an outline of the law generally as it impacts on disability. This will help to set the scene and create a knowledge base from which you can develop your understanding.

The law and disability

In general, the wide body of laws that protect all people in the United Kingdom will apply to disabled people. Such laws can include consumer law, employment law and family law. However, in certain important respects, the law that applies to disabled people, and gives an extra layer of protection is the Equality Act 2010. This law is wide ranging and incorporated many previous Acts, such as the Disability Discrimination Act, and also clearly defines discrimination. Below is a summary of the Act. However, as we go through the book continuous reference will be made to the Act as it applies to the many areas of life, such as employment and transport, that directly affects disabled people.

The Equality Act 2010

The Equality Act 2010 prohibits discrimination against people with the protected characteristics that are specified in section 4 of the Act. Disability is one of the specified protected characteristics. Protection from discrimination for disabled people applies to disabled people in a range of circumstances, covering the provision of goods, facilities and services, the exercise of public functions, premises, work, education, and associations. Only those people who are defined as disabled in accordance with section 6 of the Act, and the associated Schedules and regulations made under that section, will be entitled to the protection that the Act provides to disabled people. However, importantly, the Act also provides protection for non-disabled people who are subjected to direct discrimination or harassment because of their association with a disabled person or because they are wrongly perceived to be disabled.

The Act defines a disabled person as, simply, a person with a disability. A person has a disability for the purposes of the Act if he or she has a physical or mental impairment and the impairment has a substantial and long-term adverse effect on his or her ability to carry out normal day-to-day activities.

This means that, in general:

o   the person must have an impairment that is either physical or mental
o   the impairment must have adverse effects which are substantial
o   the substantial adverse effects must be long-term and
o   the long-term substantial adverse effects must have an effect on normal day-to-day activities

Definition of 'impairment'

The definition requires that the effects which a person may experience must arise from a physical or mental impairment. The term mental or physical impairment should be given its ordinary meaning. It is not necessary for the cause of the impairment to be established, nor does the impairment have to be the result of an illness. In many cases, there will be no dispute as to whether a person has an impairment. Any disagreement is more likely to be about whether the effects of the impairment are sufficient to fall within the definition and in particular whether they are long-term. This is a crucial fact.

Whether a person is disabled for the purposes of the Act is generally determined by reference to the effect that an impairment has on that person's ability to carry out normal day-to-day activities. An exception to this is a person with severe disfigurement. A disability can arise from a wide range of impairments which can be:

- o sensory impairments, such as those affecting sight or hearing;
- o impairments with fluctuating or recurring effects such as Rheumatoid arthritis, Myalgic encephalitis (ME), Chronic fatigue syndrome (CFS), Fibromyalgia, Depression and Epilepsy;
- o progressive, such as Motor neurone disease, Muscular dystrophy, and forms of Dementia;
- o auto-immune conditions such as Systemic lupus erythematosis (SLE);
- o organ specific, including Respiratory conditions, such as Asthma, and cardiovascular diseases, including Thrombosis, Stroke and Heart disease;
- o developmental, such as Autistic spectrum disorders (ASD), Dyslexia and Dyspraxia;
- o learning disabilities;
- o mental health conditions with symptoms such as anxiety, low mood, panic attacks, phobias, or unshared perceptions; eating disorders; bipolar affective disorders; obsessive compulsive disorders; personality disorders; post traumatic stress disorder, and some self-harming behaviour;
- o Mental illnesses, such as depression and schizophrenia;
- o produced by injury to the body, including to the brain.

Persons with HIV infection, cancer and multiple sclerosis

The Act states that a person who has cancer, HIV infection or Multiple sclerosis (MS) is a disabled person. This means that the person is protected by the Act effectively from the point of diagnosis.

Certain conditions are not regarded as impairments. These are:

o addiction to, or dependency on, alcohol, nicotine, or any other substance (other than in consequence of the substance being medically prescribed);

o the condition known as seasonal allergic rhinitis (e.g. hayfever), except where it aggravates the effect of another condition;

o tendency to set fires;

o tendency to steal;

o tendency to physical or sexual abuse of other persons;

o exhibitionism;

A person with an excluded condition may nevertheless be protected as a disabled person if he or she has an accompanying impairment which meets the requirements of the definition. For example, a person who is addicted to a substance such as alcohol may also have depression, or a physical impairment such as liver damage, arising from the alcohol addiction. While this person would not meet the definition simply on the basis of having an addiction, he or she may still meet the definition as a result of the effects of the depression or the liver damage.

Disfigurements which consist of a tattoo (which has not been removed), non-medical body piercing, or something attached through such piercing, are treated as not having a substantial adverse effect on the person's ability to carry out normal day-to-day activities.

The Act says that, except for the provisions in Part 12 (Transport) and section 190 (improvements to let dwelling houses), the provisions of the Act also apply in relation to a person who previously has had a disability as defined in the Act. This means that someone who is no longer disabled, but who met the requirements of the definition in the past, will still be covered by the Act. Also protected would be someone who continues to experience debilitating effects as a result of treatment for a past disability.

Definition of 'long-term effects'

The Act states that, for the purpose of deciding whether a person is disabled, a long-term effect of an impairment is one:

o   which has lasted at least 12 months; or
o   where the total period for which it lasts, from the time of the first onset, is likely to be at least 12 months; or
o   which is likely to last for the rest of the life of the person affected

Special provisions apply when determining whether the effects of an impairment that has fluctuating or recurring effects are long-term. Also a person who is deemed to be a disabled person does not need to satisfy the long-term requirement.

The cumulative effect of related impairments should be taken into account when determining whether the person has experienced a long-term effect for the purposes of meeting the definition of a disabled person. The substantial adverse effect of an impairment which has developed from, or is likely to develop from, another impairment should be taken into account when determining whether the effect has lasted, or is likely to last at least twelve months, or for the rest of the life of the person affected.

Normal day-to-day activities

In general, day-to-day activities are things people do on a regular or daily basis, and examples include shopping, reading and writing, having a conversation or using the telephone, watching television, getting washed and dressed, preparing and eating food, carrying out household tasks, walking and travelling by various forms of transport, and taking part in social activities. Normal day-to-day activities can include general work-related activities, and study and education-related activities, such as interacting with colleagues, following instructions, using a computer, driving, carrying out interviews, preparing written documents, and keeping to a timetable or a shift pattern.

The term 'normal day-to-day activities' is not intended to include activities which are normal only for a particular person, or a small group of people. In deciding whether an activity is a normal day-to-day activity, account should be taken of how far it is carried out by people on a daily or frequent basis. In this context, 'normal' should be given its ordinary, everyday meaning.

A normal day-to-day activity is not necessarily one that is carried out by a majority of people. For example, it is possible that some activities might be carried out only, or more predominantly, by people of a particular gender, such as breast-feeding or applying make-up, and cannot therefore be said to be normal for most people. They would nevertheless be considered to be normal day-to-day activities.

Also, whether an activity is a normal day-to-day activity should not be determined by whether it is more normal for it to be carried out at a particular time of day. For example, getting out of bed and getting dressed are activities that are normally associated with the morning. They may be carried out much later in the day by workers who work night shifts, but they would still be considered to be normal day-to-day activities. The following examples demonstrate a range of day-to-day effects on impairment:

- o Difficulty in getting dressed,
- o Difficulty carrying out activities associated with toileting, or caused by frequent minor incontinence;
- o Difficulty preparing a meal,
- o Difficulty eating;
- o Difficulty going out of doors unaccompanied, for example, because the person has a phobia, a physical restriction, or a learning disability;
- o Difficulty waiting or queuing,
- o Difficulty using transport; for example, because of physical restrictions, pain or fatigue, a frequent need for a lavatory or as a result of a mental impairment or learning disability;
- o Difficulty in going up or down steps, stairs or gradients;
- o A total inability to walk, or an ability to walk only a short distance without difficulty;
- o Difficulty entering or staying in environments that the person perceives as strange or frightening;
- o Behaviour which challenges people around the person, making it difficult for the person to be accepted in public places;
- o Persistent difficulty crossing a road safely,
- o Persistent general low motivation or loss of interest in everyday activities;
- o Difficulty accessing and moving around buildings;
- o Difficulty operating a computer, for example, because of physical restrictions in using a keyboard, a visual impairment or a learning disability;
- o Difficulty picking up and carrying objects of moderate weight, such as a bag of shopping or a small piece of luggage, with one hand;
- o Inability to converse, or give instructions orally, in the person's native spoken language;

o Difficulty understanding or following simple verbal instructions;

o Difficulty hearing and understanding another person speaking clearly over the voice telephone

o Persistent and significant difficulty in reading or understanding written material where this is in the person's native written language,

o Frequent confused behaviour, intrusive thoughts, feelings of being controlled, or delusions;

o Persistently wanting to avoid people or significant difficulty taking part in normal social interaction or forming social relationships,

o Persistent difficulty in recognising, or remembering the names of, familiar people such as family or friends;

o Persistent distractibility or difficulty concentrating;

o Compulsive activities or behaviour, or difficulty in adapting after a reasonable period to minor changes in a routine.

Whether a person satisfies the definition of a disabled person for the purposes of the Act will depend upon the full circumstances of the case. That is, whether the substantial adverse effect of the impairment on normal day-to-day activities is long term.

Specialised activities
Where activities are themselves highly specialised or involve highly specialised levels of attainment, they would not be regarded as normal day-to-day activities for most people. In some instances work-related activities are so highly specialised that they would not be regarded as normal day-to-day activities. The same is true of other specialised activities such as playing a musical instrument to a high standard of achievement; taking part in activities where very specific skills or level of ability are required; or playing a particular sport to a high level of ability, such as would be required for a

professional footballer or athlete. Where activities involve highly specialised skills or levels of attainment, they would not be regarded as normal day-to-day activities for most people.

Normal day-to-day activities also include activities that are required to maintain personal well-being or to ensure personal safety, or the safety of other people. Account should be taken of whether the effects of an impairment have an impact on whether the person is inclined to carry out or neglect basic functions such as eating, drinking, sleeping, keeping warm or personal hygiene; or to exhibit behaviour which puts the person or other people at risk.

Indirect effects

An impairment may not directly prevent someone from carrying out one or more normal day-to-day activities, but it may still have a substantial adverse effect on how the person carries out those activities. For example pain or fatigue: where an impairment causes pain or fatigue, the person may have the ability to carry out a normal day-to-day activity, but may be restricted in the way that it is carried out because of experiencing pain in doing so. Or the impairment might make the activity more than usually fatiguing so that the person might not be able to repeat the task over a sustained period of time.

Disabled children

The effects of impairments may not be apparent in babies and young children because they are too young to have developed the ability to carry out activities that are normal for older children and adults. Regulations provide that an impairment to a child under six years old is to be treated as having a substantial and long-term adverse effect on the ability of that child to carry out normal day-to-day activities where it would normally have a substantial and long-term adverse effect on the ability of a person aged six years or over to carry out normal day-to-day activities.

Children aged six and older are subject to the normal requirements of the definition. That is, that they must have an impairment which has a substantial and long-term adverse effect on their ability to carry out normal day-to-day activities. However, in considering the ability of a child aged six or over to carry out a normal day-to-day activity, it is necessary to take account of the level of achievement which would be normal for a person of a similar age.

Part 6 of the Act provides protection for disabled pupils and students by preventing discrimination against them at school or in post-16 education because of, or for a reason related to, their disability. A pupil or student must satisfy the definition of disability as described in this guidance in order to be protected by Part 6 of the Act. The duties for schools in the Act, including the duty for schools to make reasonable adjustments for disabled children, are designed to dovetail with duties under the Special Educational Needs (SEN) framework which are based on a separate definition of special educational needs. Further information on these duties can be found in the SEN Code of Practice and the Equality and Human Rights Commission's Codes of Practice for Education.

****

Useful Contacts

Gov.uk
www.gov.uk/rights-disabled-person/overview

Children's Legal Centre
University of Essex
Wivenhoe Park
Colchester CO4 3SQ
01206 714650 (advice line Mon-Fri-10-12.30 and 2-4.30 pm
www.childrenslegal centre.com

Disability Law Service
39-45 Cavell Street
London E1 2BP
0207 791 9800
www.dls.org.uk

Disability Rights Commission
DRC Helpline
Freepost
MID 02164
Stratford upon Avon CV37 9BR

Disability Rights UK
Ground Floor
CAN Mezzanine
49-51 East Rd
London N1 6AH
Tel:: 020 7250 8181
(this line open Mon-Fri, between 10.00 and 12.30pm and 1.30 and 4.00pm)

Chapter 3

Professionals and Organisations That You and Your Child Might be Involved With

When you have a disabled child, you will inevitably come into contact with a variety of different professionals from health services, social services, education and different voluntary organisations. This will continue throughout your son or daughter's childhood and early adulthood, sometimes throughout his or her life.

This can be overwhelming and in the first instance you may be confused about each persons role, how they can help you and who employs them. This chapter outlines the different roles that professionals play and how they can help you. In addition, there are a number of agencies listed where you can get all the advice and support that you need. Some of these agencies are statutory, which are the ones run by the state under legislation, such as the NHS, and some are voluntary. The one common denominator is that they all provide invaluable help and support.

People who may be involved in your childs care.

Clinical psychologist

A clinical psychologist is a health professional who helps people with specific problems with learning or behaviour difficulties.

Communication support worker

A communication support worker works alongside teachers to provide sign language support for young deaf children in nursery or school.

Dietician

A dietician is a health professional who gives advice about nutrition and swallowing or feeding difficulties.

Educational psychologist

An educational psychologist is qualified teacher who is also trained as a psychologist. They help children who find it difficult to learn or to understand or communicate with others. They can assess your child's development and provide support and advice.

General practitioner (GP)

A GP is a family doctor who works in a surgery either on their own or with other GPs. Your doctor deals with your child's general health and can refer you to clinics, hospitals and specialists when needed.

Health visitor (Health Service)

A health visitor is a registered nurse or a midwife with additional training. They visit families at home to give help, advice and practical assistance about the care of very young children. Some areas have specialist health visitors who have particular experience and expertise supporting families with a young disabled child.

Key worker

Some families have a key worker. A key worker will see you regularly and make sure you have all the information you need. They will also make sure that services from all the different areas, including health, education and social services, are well co-ordinated.

Key workers can act as a central point of contact for professionals working with your family, and make sure information about your child is shared where necessary.

'Designated' and 'non-designated' key workers

A 'non-designated' key worker is someone who is already working with a family, in another role. They take on the responsibilities of a key worker in addition to any other help or therapy they provide for the child or parents. 'Designated' key workers are employed mainly to co-ordinate information and support for families.

Learning disability nurses

Learning disability nurses are specialist nurses who work with children and adults with a learning disability and with their families. They can help you find services for your child.

Learning support assistant / teaching assistant

A learning support assistant or teaching assistant is someone who works alongside teachers. They support individual children or small groups to help them learn and take part in activities in schools or nurseries.

Named officer

A named officer is your family's contact person at the local education authority, if it issues a statement of special educational needs for your child. They manage your child's statutory assessment and write up the statement of needs.

Paediatric occupational therapist

A paediatric occupational therapist helps children with difficulties in carrying out the activities of everyday life, such as sitting in a chair, holding a spoon and fork or drinking from a cup. They carry out assessments to see if your child would benefit from using specialist equipment like adapted cups, buggies or chairs. They can also advise you on lifting and handling your child safely.

31

Paediatrician (Health Service)

A paediatrician is a doctor who specialises in working with babies and children. They are often the first point of contact for families who find out their child has an impairment or medical condition. Paediatricians may give you a diagnosis about your child's condition, answer any questions you may have and refer you to specialist services.

Paediatric neurologist

A paediatric neurologist is a doctor who specialises in how the brain works in very young children.

Physiotherapist

A physiotherapist is a health professional who specialises in physical and motor development. They can assess your child and develop a plan that might include helping your child control their head movement, sit, crawl or walk. A physiotherapist may see your child at home or in other settings, like a nursery.

Portage home visitor

An eucational professional who can come to the home of pre-school children with special educational needs and their families. Portage home visitors can come from a range of professional backgrounds. They may be teachers, therapists, nursery nurses, health visitors or volunteers with relevant experience.

School nurse

A school nurse is a medical nurse, based in a school, who provides support for children's medical needs.

Social worker (Childrens)

A social worker is a professional who provides practical help and advice about counselling, transport, home help and other services.

They are normally employed by the local council. Social workers may also be able to help you with claiming benefits or getting equipment you need at home.

Special educational needs co-ordinator (SENCO)

SENCOs are members of staff at a nursery, playgroup or school who co-ordinate special educational needs activities and services. They make sure that children who have special educational needs receive appropriate support.

****

Useful contacts

Support organisations

There are numerous support organisations that exist to help parents with disabled children. The internet has many useful sites which can direct you to specific organisations. One particulalry good site is http://www.accessiblecountryside.org.uk/organisations. They have a comprehensive list which is very helpful and detailed. Below are listed a few such organisations.

Cerebra

A unique charity set up to help improve the lives of children and young people with brain- related conditions through researching, educating and directly supporting children and their carers.
FREEPOST SWC3360
Carmarthen SA311ZY
www.cerebra.org.uk info@cerebra.org.uk 0800 3281159

Citizens Advice Bureau

Helps people resolve their legal, money and other problems by providing free, confidential and impartial information and advice. It has a number of field offices across England. Myddelton House,
115-123 Pentonville Road,
London N1 9LZ
www.citizensadvice.org.uk (local offices)
www.adviceguide.org.uk
020 78332181 (admin only)

Contact a Family

A UK-wide charity providing support, advice and information for families with children with additional needs. It runs a helpline for family members and can help you get in touch with other parents of disabled children living near you.

209-211 City Road
London
EC1V 1JN
www.cafamily.org.uk
helpline@cafamily.org.uk
0808 8083555 or 020 76088700

Council for Disabled Children

A national forum for the discussion, development and dissemination of a wide range of policy and practice issues relating to service provision for children and young people with disabilities and special educational needs. Membership is drawn from a wide range of professional, voluntary and statutory organisations and includes parent representatives and representatives of disabled people.

8 Wakley Street
London
EC1V 7QE
www.councilfordisabledchildren.org.uk
cdc@ncb.org.uk
020 78431900

Daycare Trust

A national childcare charity working to promote high-quality, affordable childcare for everyone. It provides information about all aspects of childcare.

2nd Floor, The Bridge
73-81 Southwark Bridge Road
London
SE1 0NQ
www.daycaretrust.org.uk; www.payingforchildcare.org.uk
info@daycaretrust.org.uk
020 79407528 (admin only)

Department for Education

The Department for Education is responsible for education and children's services in England. We work to achieve a highly educated society in which opportunity is equal for children and young people, no matter what their background or family circumstances. DfE is a ministerial department, supported by 9 agencies and public bodies.
Ministerial and Public Communications Division
Department for Education
Piccadilly Gate
Store Street
Manchester M1 2WD
https://www.gov.uk/government/organisations/department-for-education
0370 000 2288

Disability Rights UK

A national, pan-disability organisation led by disabled people. It provides advice, publications and a number of helplines for disabled people.
12 City Forum
250 City Road
London EC1V 8AF
www.disabilityrightsuk.org
skill4disabledstudents@disabilityrightsuk.org
Disabled students helpline: 0800 3285050
Independent living advice line: 0845 0264748
Admin line: 020 72503222

Family Information Service (FIS)

The FIS can give you information about the full range of childcare and other services for children, young people and families available in the area. You can contact the FIS through your local authority office or find you local FIS contact details at the following website. www.daycaretrust.org.uk/findyourFIS

Information Advice and Support Services Network (IASSN)

The Information, Advice and Support Services Network (IASS Network) provide training and support to local Information Advice and Support (IAS) Services across England. The IASS Network was previously known as the National Parent Partnership Network (NPPN), who undertook a similar role with local Parent Partnership Services.

Information, Advice and Support Services Network

Council for Disabled Children
8 Wakley Street
London
EC1V 7QE
http://www.iassnetwork.org.uk/
iassn@ncb.org.uk

Mencap

The Royal MENCAP Society is a registered charity that offers services to children, young people and adults with learning disabilities. It offers help and advice on benefits, housing and employment. It also offers help and advice to anyone with any other issues, or will direct them to the right place. It can also provide information and support for leisure, recreational services (Gateway Clubs), residential services and holidays.

123 Golden Lane
London
EC1Y 0RT
www.mencap.org.uk

help@mencap.org.uk
0808 8081111 or 020 74540454

NHS Direct

A 24-hour nurse advice and health information service, providing confidential information on what to do if you or a family member is feeling ill, have particular health conditions, or need local healthcare services or self-help and support organisations.
www.nhsdirect.nhs.uk
0845 6064647

The Royal National Institute of Blind People (RNIB)

RNIB is the leading charity offering information, support and advice to almost two million people with sight loss. It has practical ways to help those living with sight loss, including advice about travelling, shopping, managing money and finances, and technology for blind and partially sighted people.

105 Judd Street
London
WC1H 9NE
www.rnib.org.uk
helpline@rnib.org.uk
0303 1239999

Scope

Scope is the UK's leading disability charity. Its focus is on children, young people and adults with cerebral palsy and people living with other severe and complex impairments. Its vision is a world where disabled people have the same opportunities to fulfill their life ambitions as non-disabled people.

6 Market Road
London
N7 9PW
www.scope.org.uk response@scope.org.uk
0808 8003333 Text: SCOPE plus message to 80039

Sense

The major UK voluntary organisation for children, young people and adults born with multi- sensory impairment (MSI) and their families. The website has information about the help and services available to people with MSI, their families and professionals.
101 Pentonville Road
London N1 9LG
www.sense.org.uk
info@sense.org.uk
0845 1270066

Transition Information Network (TIN)

The network is hosted by the Council for Disabled Children. The aim of the website is to provide information to parents and practitioners about disabled young people's transition to adulthood. There is also a young people's section with information, news and events.
c/o Council for Disabled Children
8 Wakley Street
London
EC1V 7QE
www.transitioninfonetwork.org.uk
tin@ncb.org.uk
020 78436006

****

Chapter 4

Finances-The Benefits System

Having looked at the role of the professional and also useful organisations, in this chapter we will look at the rights of the disabled child and the rights of their parents in relation to the benefit system. The whole range of welfare benefits available and also entitlements is contained within Appendix 1. However, for the purposes of this chapter we will start with the period of pregnancy. Pregnancy and maternity is now one of the protected characteristics in the Equality Act 2010 and there is implied into every woman's term of employment a maternity equality clause (s 73 Equality Act 2010). The Act protects women from direct discrimination (s 13(1)) and indirect discrimination (s 19(1)) in relation to pregnancy and maternity.

Right to maternity leave

All pregnant employees are entitled to 52 weeks maternity leave. This consists of 26 weeks Ordinary Maternity Leave and 26 weeks Additional Maternity Leave. This is available to all employees from the first day of employment. The employee can choose when they start their leave but the earliest it can start is 10 weeks before the baby is due. The only women not entitled to maternity leave are:

o   Share fisherwomen
o   Women who normally work abroad (unless they have a work connection with the UK)
o   Policewomen and women serving in the armed forces

Compulsory maternity leave

An employer may not permit an employee to work during her compulsory maternity period. Compulsory maternity leave is a period of two weeks commencing on the day on which childbirth occurs. An employer who allows a pregnant person to work can be fined.

Giving notice to the employer

In order to qualify for maternity leave the employer must be informed by the end of the 15th week before the baby is due:

- o that the employee is pregnant
- o the week in which the baby is expected; and
- o the date when the employee intends to start ordinary maternity leave.

There is no obligation to put this in writing unless asked to. However, it is a good idea to do so. Once the employer has been informed that maternity leave will be taken they have 28 days to inform you when maternity leave starts.

If the employee already has a contractual right to maternity pay/leave, she may exercise her right to the more favourable terms. If there is a redundancy situation during the leave period and it is not practicable because of the redundancy for the employer to continue to employ her under her existing contract, she is entitled to be offered a suitable vacancy before her employment ends. If a woman intends to return to work before the end of maternity leave, 56 days notice must be given. Since women who qualify now have the right to take Additional Maternity Leave, and there is no obligation to notify the employer during the initial notification, then until notification of a return to work is given, the women will retain the right to return but not pay.

Work during the maternity leave period

Regulation 12A provides that an employee may carry out up to ten days work for her employer during her statutory maternity period (excluding the compulsory maternity period) without bringing her maternity period to an end.

Time off for Ante-natal care

To qualify for this right the employee must have made an appointment for ante-natal care on the advice of a doctor, midwife or health visitor. The employer may not refuse time off for the first visit, but for further appointments, the employer may ask for a certificate or appointment card or other evidence.

Statutory Maternity Pay

The Social Security Act of 1996 and the Statutory Maternity Pay regulations of the same year entitle certain employees to statutory maternity pay. This has been amended by the 2002 Employment Act. SMP is paid for a maximum of 39 weeks. For the first six weeks of maternity leave SMP is paid at 90% of the average gross weekly earnings (before tax and NI) for the remaining 33 weeks it is paid at 90% of gross weekly earnings or £139.58 a week (2015-2016) whichever is the lower. To claim SMP, a person must tell their employer, 28 days before maternity leave, that they are pregnant and will be off work because of birth. A medical certificate has to be provided.

When is SMP paid?

How long SMP is paid for depends on when the baby is due. It is paid up to 39 weeks. The earliest a person can start maternity leave and start to get SMP is 11 weeks before the baby is due. The latest date to start maternity leave and receiving SMP is the week after the week when the baby is born. If a person is sick with a pregnancy related illness before the baby is due, SMP will start the week following the week that sickness began. If a person is sick with a non-pregnancy related illness they can claim Statutory Sick pay until the week that the baby is due.

Maternity Allowance

If an employee is not entitled to get SMP they may be entitled to maternity allowance instead. This is administered through Jobcentre Plus and a person might get maternity benefit if:

- they are employed, but not eligible for SMP
- they are registered self-employed and paying class C National Insurance Contributions (NIC's) or hold a Small Earnings Exemption Certificate
- they have been very recently employed or self-employed.

Further, they may be eligible if:

- they have been employed or self-employed for at least 26 weeks in the 'test period' (66 weeks up to and including the week before the week the baby is due) part weeks count as full weeks; and
- they earned £30 a week averaged over any 13 week period in the test period.

Returning to work after maternity leave

There is an automatic right to return to work after maternity leave and it is assumed the person will do so unless they state otherwise. If a person decides to return earlier than the date notified by the employer, then at least 56 days notice must be given of returning.

Parental leave

The Maternity and Parental Leave Regulations 1999 provide that every person who cares for a young child, or has recently adopted a child, can take time off from work at his or her own convenience to care for that child. Minimum provisions are set for leave, preconditions are set for leave and the notice that an employee has to give an employer before leave can be taken is set out. Employers and employees can agree to vary these provisions by using a workforce agreement as long as it is equal to or more favorable than the statutory provisions.

Any employee who has one year's continuous employment at the date the leave is due to start, and who has, or expects to have, responsibility for a child at that time can apply to take parental leave. A person will have responsibility for a child under the regulations if he/she has parental responsibility under the Children Act 1989 or is registered as the father under the provision of the Births and Deaths Register Act. The leave entitlement is up to 4 weeks unpaid parental leave per year while the child is under the age of 5, subject to an overall maximum of 18 weeks leave in respect of each child. If there are twins, each parent can take 26 weeks parental leave. The leave for the parent of a disabled child is 18 weeks per child. the leave for parents of an adopted child is 18 weeks up to their 18th birthday or 5th anniversary of their adoption, whichever comes first.

Employers can request records of leave already taken with previous employers; the entitlement is per child and not per employer. The employee can take leave in blocks of 1 week (or blocks of one day where the child is disabled) to a maximum of 4 weeks in respect of an individual child in an individual year. (Part time employees get a pro-rata entitlement.)

Paternity leave

In addition, the Employment Act 2002 widened the scope and range of paternity leave. The Act introduced the right to two weeks paid leave in addition to the 13 weeks unpaid leave. This became effective from April 2003. Leave must be taken within 8 weeks of the birth of the child or placement of the child through adoption. For employees to claim paternity leave they must:

o Be employed and have worked for their employer for at least 26 weeks before the end of the 15th week before the expected week of childbirth; and

o Be the biological father of the child, or be married to or be the partner of the baby's mother (this includes same sex partners, whether or not they are registered civil partners); and

o Have some responsibility for the child's upbringing; and

o Have given the employer the correct notice to take paternity leave.

o Paternity leave can be taken as a single block of either one or two weeks.

All terms and conditions of employment remain intact during the period of paternity leave except the right to remuneration. Employees are entitled to return to the jobs they had before they took paternity leave.

The Additional Paternity Leave Regulations 2010

The Additional Paternity Leave Regulations 2010 recognised that mothers can often be the main earner for the family and aims to promote shared parenting. The regulations enabled eligible employees to have the right to take additional paternity leave and pay. However the right only affected parents of children that were due to be born on or after the 3rd April 2011 or where one or both of the parents had received adoptive notification on or after the 3rd April 2011 that they have been matched with a child for adoption.

Additional Paternity Leave (APL) allowed a father to take up to 26 weeks leave to care for a child and also allowed mothers to 'transfer' up to 6 months of maternity leave to their partner. APL started 20 weeks after the birth of the child and ended no later then the child's first birthday. However, Additional Paternity Leave is to be replaced by Shared parental leave for babies born on or after

April 5th 2015. Therefore, for the purposes of this book we will refer to the new regulations outlined below.

Shared parental leave

Shared parental leave is available for babies with an expected week of childbirth (EWC) starting on or after 5 April 2015. The new right is governed by the Shared Parental Leave Regulations 2014, in force from 1 December 2014. The following deals with the main features of the draft regulations; the detail could, of course, change when the final regulations are published.

A woman, who is eligible for shared parental leavel has the right to bring her maternity leave and pay period to an end early and convert the outstanding period of maternity leave and pay into a period of shared parental leave and pay that can be taken by either parent. Shared parental leave can be taken in a more flexible way than maternity leave. It does not have to be a single continuous period; leave periods can be as little as a week and both parents can be absent from work at the same time.

Shared parental leave must be taken before the child's first birthday and is in addition to the right to unpaid parental leave under the Maternity and Parental Leave Regulations 1999. The existing right to additional paternity leave is replaced by the new right to shared parental leave, although remains in place for babies with an EWC starting before 5 April 2015.

A parent taking adoption leave also has the right to convert a period of adoption leave into a period of shared parental leave which either parent can take in a flexible way if they have a matching date on or after 5 April 2015. Below are the main points of the new regulations:

o The right to shared parental leave applies to babies with an expected week of childbirth starting on or after 5 April 2015. The default position remains that a woman is entitled to 52 weeks' maternity leave and 39 weeks' maternity pay.

- o However, a woman on maternity leave can commit to bringing her maternity leave and pay period to an end early. The balance of the maternity leave and pay period becomes available for either parent to take as shared parental leave and pay.
- o Shared parental leave can be taken in periods of a week or multiples of a week at a time.
- o A parent can take a period of shared parental leave at the same time that the other parent is on maternity leave or shared parental leave
- o A parent will only qualify to take shared parental leave if the other parent meets basic work and earnings criteria and the parent taking the leave meets the individual eligibility criteria (such as having 26 weeks' continuous service at the 15th week before the EWC and remaining in the same employment).
- o An employer must have at least eight weeks' notice of any period of shared parental leave.
- o Each parent can make up to three requests for periods of shared parental leave. Whether the employer can refuse a request depends on whether the employee has asked for a continuous or discontinuous period of leave.
- o Shared parental leave has to be taken before the child's first birthday

Rights during a period of shared parental leave mirror those of a woman on maternity leave: all terms and conditions of employment continue except those relating to remuneration.

If employees suffer any detrimental treatment or are dismissed as a result of taking or asking to take shared parental leave they can bring a complaint to the employment tribunal.

Adoption leave and pay

The 2002 Employment Act creates a right for parents to take

adoption leave when permanently adopting a child. An adoptive parent is entitled to take 26 weeks paid adoption leave (known as 'ordinary adoption leave') and up to 26 weeks unpaid adoption leave During ordinary adoption leave, employees will be entitled to receive Statutory Adoption Pay (SAP) for 39 weeks of £139.58 per week (2015-2016) or 90% of earnings, whichever is the lower. You should check with the DTI or DSS for current rates.

Qualifying requirements

To be entitled to take adoption leave, employees must have attained 26 weeks service with their employer at the date the adoption takes place. Leave can be taken at any time after the adoption placement begins. Employees will be required to provide evidence of the adoption to the employer. Only one partner in a couple will be able to take adoption leave. The other partner, male or female, will be able to take paternity leave for 2 weeks and receive SPP. There are statutory notice provisions covering how and when employees must inform employers that they wish to take adoption leave. These are flexible and can be verified with the employer.

During the period of ordinary adoption leave the employee is entitled to all their terms and conditions, except the right to remuneration. During the period of additional adoption leave, the employee is in the same position as someone on additional maternity leave — namely that whilst most of the terms and conditions of employment will be suspended, those relating to notice, confidentiality, implied terms of mutual trust and confidence, redundancy terms and disciplinary and grievance procedures will remain in place.

The right to return after either ordinary or additional adoption leave mirror's the provisions for ordinary and additional maternity leave respectively.

Other benefits available if your child is disabled

From birth, you should register your child with the local authority social care department. You can also apply to the authority for an assessment of your child's special needs. If your child is registered as blind you can apply for:

o A disabled child premium in the assessment of your housing benefit and health benefits and a disabled child element with your tax credit. If you are claiming universal credit, the higher rate of the disabled child addition will be included in your calculation.

o You can also get a 50% reduction in your TV licence if you transfer the licence into the child's name.

Working Tax Credits and children

If you are responsible for a child or young person, you can get Working Tax Credit provided you work at least 16 hours a week if you're single, or at least 24 hours between you if you're in a couple, with one of you working at least 16 hours a week. Some couples with children may qualify without working for 24 hours between them, provided one of them works 16 hours. Your income also needs to be low enough. A child is someone under 16, and a young person is someone who is 16, 17, 18 or 19 and still in full-time education up to A level or equivalent, or on certain approved training courses. You are responsible for a child or young person if they normally live with you or you have main responsibility for their care. You cannot usually get Working Tax Credit if your child is in local authority care.

You may be able to get Working Tax Credit for a short period after your child is 16 or leaves school, depending on when their birthday is and what they do on leaving school.

If you are on maternity leave, paternity leave or adoption leave and you normally work 16 hours or more, you can claim Working

Tax Credit before you go back to work, as long as you are responsible for a child. If it is your first baby and you are not responsible for any other children, you will have to wait until the child is born, or comes to live with you before you can claim.

Income levels and Working Tax Credits

Even if you meet the work conditions, you will only get Working Tax Credit if you have a low enough income. Your income for tax credits is assessed on an annual basis. Whether or not you get Working Tax Credit, and how much you get, depends on your income and your circumstances. Not all your income will be taken into account (for example, maintenance and child support, most Statutory Maternity, Paternity or Adoption Pay and all Maternity Allowance paid to you is ignored). Usually, HM Revenue and Customs (HMRC) will use your income for the previous tax year to work out what you are due.

Working Tax Credit rates

The maximum Working Tax Credit you can get is calculated by adding together different elements which are based on your circumstances. There is a basic element which is included for anyone who is entitled to Working Tax Credit. There is a second adult element if you are claiming as a member of a couple although there are some circumstances where a couple will not get this. You have to claim as a couple if you live with a partner. This includes a partner of the opposite or same sex. There is a lone parent element if you are a lone parent.

There is a 30 hour element if you work at least 30 hours a week (or if you are claiming as a couple with a child and you jointly work at least 30 hours). There is a disability element if you are disabled, get certain benefits and you work at least 16 hours a week. You can also get a disability element if your partner qualifies for it or two disability elements if you both qualify.

There is a severe disability element if you get the highest rate care component of Disability Living Allowance, the enhanced rate of the daily living component of Personal Independence Payment, the higher rate of Attendance Allowance, or Armed Forces Independence Payment. You will get two severe disability elements if you and your partner both qualify.

You may also be able to get a childcare element. This is equivalent to up to 70% of childcare costs provided by a registered childminder, out-of-school club or another approved provider. There is a limit on the maximum eligible weekly childcare cost which means that the most this element can be is 70% of the maximum.

Rates of Working Tax Credit

Element of Working Tax Credit	Maximum annual amount from 6 April 2014	Maximum annual amount from 6 April 2015
Basic element	£1,940	£1,960
Second adult element	£1,990	£2,010
Lone parent element	£1,990	£2,010
30 hour element	£800	£810
Disability element	£2,935	£2,970
Severe disability element	£1,255	£1,275

Childcare element (up to 70% of the maximum):	Maximum weekly amount from 6 April 2014	Maximum weekly amount from 6 April 2015
Maximum weekly eligible cost for one child	£175 (maximum payable £122)	£175 (maximum payable £122)
Maximum weekly eligible cost for two or more children	£300 (maximum payable £210)	£300 (maximum payable £210)

To apply for Working Tax Credit, contact the Tax Credit helpline for an application pack. The application form for your first claim is Form TC600. The helpline number is 0345 300 3900 (textphone 0345 300 3909).

When you apply for Working Tax Credit, you will have to provide your national insurance number. You will normally also have to give the national insurance number of any partner who lives with you. If you don't know your national insurance number, but you think you have one, try to provide information that will help the office find your number. If you do not have a national insurance number, you will have to apply for one.

You may be able to get some Working Tax Credit for a period before you apply, if you met the conditions and could have claimed earlier. You can normally only get Working Tax Credit backdated for a maximum of 31 days before the date you apply.

If you are refused Working Tax Credit and think you are entitled, or that the amount you are awarded is wrong, call the Tax Credits Helpline and ask HM Revenue and Customs (HMRC) to explain their decision. If you are not satisfied with the explanation, you can make a formal request for the decision to be looked at again. This is called a mandatory reconsideration. You must ask for a reconsideration within 30 days of the date of the decision. If you are not satisfied with the result of the reconsideration, you can then appeal to an independent tribunal.

It's against the law for you to be treated unfairly because of your race, sex, disability, sexuality, religion or belief when HMRC decide about your Working Tax Credit claim. Also, HMRC has a policy which says they will not discriminate against you because of other things, such as if you've got HIV or if you have caring responsibilities. If you feel that you've been discriminated against, you can make a complaint about this.

Other help when you get Working Tax Credit

When you get Working Tax Credit, you may be entitled to other financial help. If you pay rent, you may be able to get Housing

Benefit. If you have to pay Council Tax, you may be able to get Council Tax Reduction. Being on Working Tax Credit may also give you access to other help. For example, you may be entitled to health benefits, including free prescriptions. You may also be able get help with the costs of a new baby from a Sure Start maternity grant or help with the costs of a funeral from a funeral payment. Whether or not you can get this help will depend on your income, whether you get a disability element with your Working Tax Credit and whether you also get Child Tax Credit.

Additional help-Family Fund

You can get help from the Family Fund with some of the additional costs arising from the child's disability. the purpose of this fund is to help families with the day-to-day care of a severely disabled child through the provision of grants and information concerning care. the Family Fund is an independent charity and is financed by the government.

You can receive help from the fund if you are providing care at home for a severely disabled child under the age of 18 and are entitled to tax credits and certain other benefits. You cannot get help for a child in Local Authority care.

The help that the Family Fund can provide is:

o Holidays or leisure activities for the whole family
o Washing machine and dryer for extra washing arising from caring for a child
o Bedding and clothing if there is additional wear and tear.
o IT equipment
o Play equipment related to your child's special needs.

The first step is to contact the Family Fund by phone or online as follows:

Tel: 0844 974 4099

Online www.familyfund.org.uk

Usually the first step after contact is to receive a visit from a representative of the Fund.

Loans and grants to assist in the care of a disabled child

If you have been receiving Income Support, Income Related Employment and Support Allowance, Income Based Job Seekers Allowance or Pension Credit for at least 26 weeks you may be eligible for a budgeting loan to help meet one off costs. You need to contact your local authority to obtain more details.

Home adaptations

You may be eligible for adaptations in the home, including a Disabled Facilities Grant You should contact your local authority for more information.

Healthy Start Vouchers

The Healthy Start Scheme provides vouchers for fresh milk, infant formula milk and fresh or frozen fruit and vegetables. It also provides coupons to claim free vitamin supplements without a prescription. There are certain criteria for eligibility:

- You must be at least ten weeks pregnant and under 18 and not subject to immigration control
- You are at least ten weeks pregnant or have a child under 4 and you or a member of your family receive income-related employment and support allowance , income support, income based job seekers allowance or child tax credit and your income is below £16,190. You can get more information about Healthy Start on the Healthy Start Helpline 0845 607 6823 or from the website www.healthystart.nhs.uk

There may be help also through the Nursery Milk Scheme, which is available for children under 5 who attend approved day care facilities for two or more hours a day and also some 4 year olds in reception classes. For more information go to www.nurserymilk.co.uk.

Disability Living Allowance-Care Component

For a child you can be paid care component when they reach three months of age. There are situations when you can claim beforehand. If your baby is terminally ill they will automatically qualify for the highest rate of DLA as soon as you claim DLA after birth. If your baby is awarded DLA you may get a disabled child premium included in the assessment of housing and health benefits and also in the assessment of your child tax credit (see below) or in the assessment of Universal Credit. Other benefits may be enhanced. Contact your local Jobcentre Plus for details.

As the child develops the following will apply:

o From 2 years of age you can claim Vaccine damage payment. This scheme provides a tax-free lump sum for someone who is, or was immediately before death severely disabled as a result of vaccination against specific diseases. For full details of the scheme including definitions you should contact: the Vaccine Damage Payments Unit, Palatine House, Lancaster House, Preston, Lancs PR1 1HB. Tel: 01772 899 944 or go to www.gov.uk/vaccine-damage-payment.

o Your child will be eligible for a Special Educational Needs Assessment-Local Authorities in England and Wales have a duty to identify any child who might have special educational needs. You should contact your local authority for details.

o   You may also be able to apply for a Blue badge parking concession (see chapter on transport) once the child reaches 2 years of age. You can also apply for a child under 2 if there is a need to transport bulky equipment arising from the child's disability.

o   As mentioned above, from 3 years of age, you can apply for the higher rate of DLA.

o   From 5 years of age the child can be awarded a DLA lower rate component.

o   From 5 years of age the child will be eligible for free school meals, dependant on the benefits you receive and savings. School clothing grants and travel concessions may also be available.

o   From 8 years of age, if your child has to travel more than 3 miles to school they can receive help. For a disabled child you may get help even if the distance is less than 3 miles.

o   From the age of 16 years old a disabled child has the option of claiming for benefits in their own rights.

o   Other help is available, as outlined in Chapter 2, such as carer's allowance, low income benefits, housing benefits, council tax support and help with mortgage and interest costs. there is also help with home adaptations (outlined in chapter   ) help with child support and help from the family fund.

Eligibility for child benefit

All people can get child benefit if they have responsibility for a dependant child (under 16) or a qualifying young person (under 20 and in full time non-advanced education-more than 12 hours a week at school or college or approved education which is non-waged)). You have to pass the residence test and not be subject to immigration control. You do not have to be the parent or stay-at-home guardian.

You won't be eligible for child benefit if the child or young person is in local authority care or in detention for more than 8 weeks, although their are exceptions to this. You will not be eligible if you are a foster parent and get an allowance to look after the child or prospective adopter of a child placed with you by a local authority. In addition, if the young person is married, in a civil partnership or cohabiting you won't be eligible. However, special rules will apply if the child if the child is in residential accommodation provided for them because of their disability.

Guardians allowance

This is a tax free benefit for someone who is looking after someone who is effectively an orphan. You can get guardians allowance for someone who is not your birth child or adopted child and both parents of the child are dead, or one is dead and the other is missing, divorced or had their civil partnership dissolved and liable for neither maintenance or custody of the child, serving a prison sentence of more than 2 years from the date that the other parent dies or detained in hospital under sections of the Mental Health Act 1983 or other associated legislation.

The current rates of child benefit and guardians allowance

The current rates of child benefit (2015/16) are:

Only/eldest child or qualifying young person-£20.70 per week
Subsequent children £13.70

Guardians allowance-£16.55 per week.

For more information on child benefit and how to claim you should contact the Child Benefit helpline on 0300 200 3100: textphone 0300 200 3103 (there are other rules governing the payment of child benefit. Child benefit is administered by HMRC and full details of the rules governing payment and eligibility can be obtained from them via their website hmrc.gov.uk).

Carers allowance

The main welfare benefit for carers is called Carer's Allowance and it's worth £62.10 per week if you're eligible. You don't have to be related to or live with the person you care for to claim Carer's Allowance. You'll also get National Insurance credits each week towards your pension if you're under pension age.

You may not think of yourself as a carer. Perhaps you've looked after someone for a long time without ever calling yourself one, or maybe you think the help you give your spouse or parent is simply what you should be doing. If so, you may have been missing out on the help that is available to you.

To claim Carer's Allowance, you must:

- spend at least 35 hours a week caring for a disabled person - you don't have to live with them
- care for someone who receives the higher- or middle-rate care component of Disability Living Allowance, either rate of Personal Independence Payment daily living component, or any rate of Attendance Allowance
- not earn more than £102 a week (after deductions)
- not be in full-time education.

Carer's Allowance may not be paid if you're receiving a State Pension or certain other benefits, but it's still worth claiming because you could get extra Pension Credit and/or Housing Benefit.

If you're claiming Universal Credit You may be able to get an extra amount because of your caring role without having to apply for Carer's Allowance. (see below for universal credit).

If you want to make a claim for carers allowance call the Carer's Allowance Unit on 0845 608 4321 (textphone: 0845 604 5312) to request a claim pack. Or you can visit GOV.UK to download a claim form or make a claim online.

For more details concerning the range of welfare benefits generally please see appendix 1.

****

Useful contacts

Attendance Allowance helpline 0845 605 6055 or 0345 605 6055 (textphone: 0845 604 5312)

Carer's Allowance Unit 0845 608 4321 (textphone: 0845 604 5312)

DWP Bereavement Service:

Telephone: 0845 606 0265
Textphone: 0845 606 0285

Department for Work and pensions (DWP) on 0800 917 2222 (textphone 0800 917 777).

Winter Fuel Payments Helpline 0845 915 1515

Disability benefits Advice
www.gov.uk/disability-benefits-helpline

Jobcentre Plus 0800 055 6688 textphone 0800 023 4888

Pension Credit claim line 0800 99 1234 (textphone: 0800 169 0133).

Royal National Institute for the Blind 0303 123 9999
www.rnib.org.uk.

Tax Credit helpline 0345 300 3900 (textphone 0345 300 3909).

TV Licence concessions 0300 790 6165

Universal Credit helpline 0845 600 0723 (textphone 0845 600 0743).

Child benefit helpline 0300 200 3100: textphone 0300 200 3103

Family Fund 0844 974 4099 Online www.familyfund.org.uk

Healthy Start Helpline 0845 607 6823 www.healthystart.nhs.uk

www.nurserymilk.co.uk.

****

Chapter 5

Disabled People and Education

Education and the law

It's against the law for a school or other education provider to treat disabled students unfavourably. This includes: 'direct discrimination', eg refusing admission to a student because of disability; 'indirect discrimination', eg only providing application forms in one format that may not be accessible; 'discrimination arising from a disability', eg a disabled pupil is prevented from going outside at break time because it takes too long to get there; 'harassment', eg a teacher shouts at a disabled student for not paying attention when the student's disability stops them from easily concentrating and victimisation, eg suspending a disabled student because they've complained about harassment.

Reasonable adjustments

As with employers, an education provider has a duty to make 'reasonable adjustments' to make sure disabled students are not discriminated against. These changes could include changes to physical features, eg creating a ramp so that students can enter a classroom, providing extra support and aids (like specialist teachers or equipment)

Portage

It is worth at this point mentioning portage, which can benefit your child pre-school. Portage is a home-visiting educational service for pre-school children with additional support needs and their families. Portage Home Visitors are employed by Local Authorities and Charities to support children and families within their local community. The Portage model of learning is characterised by the following attributes:

- regular home visiting;
- supporting the development of play, communication, relationships, and learning for young children within the family;
- supporting the child and family's participation and inclusion in the community in their own right;
- working together with parents within the family, with them taking the leading role in the partnership that is established;
- helping parents to identify what is important to them and their child and plan goals for learning and participation;
- keeping a shared record of the child's progress and other issues raised by the family;
- responding flexibly to the needs of the child and family when providing support;
- You can find out more about Portage by contacting The National Portage Association address at the end of the chapter.

Special Educational Needs (SEN)

All publicly-funded pre-schools, nurseries, state schools and local authorities must try to identify and help assess children with Special Educational Needs. If a child has a statement of special educational needs, they should have a 'transition plan' drawn up in Year 9. This helps to plan what support the child will have after leaving school.

Higher education

All universities and higher education colleges should have a person in charge of disability issues that you can talk to about the support they offer. You can also ask local social services for an assessment to help with your day-to-day living needs.

Children with special educational needs (SEN)

Special educational needs (SEN) that affect a child's ability to learn can include their:

- o behaviour or ability to socialise, eg not being able to make friends, reading and writing, eg they have dyslexia, ability to understand things, concentration levels, eg they have Attention Deficit Hyperactivity Disorder, physical needs or impairments

If you think your child may have special educational needs, contact the 'SEN co-ordinator', or 'SENCO' in your child's school or nursery. Contact your local council if your child isn't in a school or nursery. Your local Information, Advice and Support (IAS) Service can give you advice about SEN.

Support a child can receive

A child may be eligible for SEN support - support given in school, eg speech therapy, an education, health and care plan (EHC) - a plan of care for children and young people aged up to 25 who have more complex needs. If you or your child got support before September 2014 this will continue until your local council changes to SEN support or an EHC plan.

Special educational needs support

Your child will get special educational needs (SEN) support at their school or college. Your child may need an EHC plan if they need more support than their school provides.

Children under 5
SEN support for children under 5 includes:

- o a written progress check when your child is 2 years old
- o a child health visitor carrying out a health check for your child if they're aged 2 to 3

- a written assessment in the summer term of your child's first year of primary school
- making reasonable adjustments for disabled children, eg providing aids like tactile signs

Nurseries, playgroups and childminders registered with Ofsted follow the Early Years Foundation Stage (EYFS) framework. The framework makes sure that there is support in place for children with SEN.

Children between 5 and 15

Talk to the teacher or the SEN coordinator (SENCO) if you think your child needs:

- a special learning programme
- extra help from a teacher or assistant
- to work in a smaller group
- observation in class or at break
- help taking part in class activities
- extra encouragement in their learning, eg to ask questions or to try something they find difficult
- help communicating with other children
- support with physical or personal care difficulties, eg eating, getting around school safely or using the toilet

Young people aged 16 or over in further education

Contact the college or academy before your child starts further education to make sure that they can meet your child's needs. The college and your local authority will talk to your child about the support they need.

Independent support for children of all ages

Independent supporters can help you and your child through the new SEN assessment process, including:

o replacing a statement of special educational needs with a new education, health and care plan (EHCP)

o moving a child from a learning difficulty assessment (LDA) to EHCP

Extra help

An Education, health and care (EHC) plan is for children and young people aged up to 25 who need more support than is available through special educational needs support.

EHC plans identify educational, health and social needs and set out the additional support to meet those needs.

Requesting an EHC assessment

You can ask your local authority to carry out an assessment if you think your child needs an EHC plan. A request can also be made by anyone at your child's school, a doctor, a health visitor or a nursery worker. A local authority has 6 weeks to decide whether or not to carry out an EHC assessment. If they decide to carry out an assessment you may be asked for any reports from your child's school, nursery or childminder, doctors' assessments of your child, a letter from you about your child's needs.

You'll usually find out within 16 weeks whether or not an EHC plan is going to be made for your child.

Creating an EHC plan

Your local authority will create a draft EHC plan and send you a copy. You have 15 days to comment, including if you want to ask that your child goes to a specialist needs school or specialist college.

Your local authority has 20 weeks from the date of the assessment to give you the final EHC plan.

Disagreeing with a decision

You can challenge your local authority about their decision to not carry out an assessment, their decision to not create an EHC plan, the special educational support in the EHC plan, the school named in the EHC plan. If you can't resolve the problem with your local authority, you can appeal to the special educational needs and disability tribunal.

Personal budgets

You may be able to get a personal budget for your child if they have an education, health and care (EHC) plan or have been told that they need an EHC plan. It allows you to have a say in how to spend the money on support for your child. There are 3 ways you can use your personal budget. You can have:

○ direct payments made into your account - you buy and manage services yourself

○ an arrangement with your local authority or school where they hold the money for you but you still decide how to spend it (sometimes called 'notional arrangements')

○ third-party arrangements - you choose someone else to manage the money for you

You can have a combination of all 3 options

If your child got support before September 2014

Your child will continue to get support until they're moved across to special educational needs (SEN) support or an education, health and care (EHC) plan. Your child should move to:

○ SEN Support by summer 2015 if they already get help through School Action, School Action Plus, Early Years Action or Early Years Action Plus

- o an EHC plan by spring 2018 if they have a statement
- o an EHC plan by September 2016 if they have an LDA

Your school will tell you when they plan to move your child to SEN support and your council will tell you when they are going to transfer your child to an EHC plan.

Early Years Action and School Action

This support is either a different way of teaching certain things, or some help from an extra adult.

Early Years Action Plus and School Action Plus

This is extra help from an external specialist, eg a speech therapist.

Assessments

An assessment of special educational needs involves experts and people involved in your child's education. They ask about your child's needs and what should be done to meet them.

Statement

A statement of special education needs describes your child's needs and how they should be met, including what school they should go to.

Further education

If your child has a statement of special educational needs, they'll have a 'transition plan' drawn up in Year 9. This helps to plan for their future after leaving school.

Disabled people and financing studies

Financial support for all students comes in the form of tuition fee loans, means tested loans for living expenses and also a range of supplementary grants and loans depending on individual circumstances. Entitlement to student support depends on where you are living and where you intend to study. For details of loan entitlement and rates also Bursaries, you should contact:

Student finance England if you reside in England-0845 300 5090
www.gov.uk/student-finance

Northern Ireland Student finance NI 0845 600 0662
www.studentfinanceni.co.uk

Scotland Student Awards Agency for Scotland 0300 555 0505
www.saas.gov.uk

Wales Student Finance Wales 0845 602 8845
www.studentfianncewales.co.uk

For details of loans and bursaries plus other sources of finance, you should contact the student support officer responsible for advice at the educational institution that you are to attend.

Students and means tested benefits
If you are a disabled student and want more information on benefits entitlement and how being a student in higher education affects benefits then you should contact the Disability Advisor at your local Jobcentre Plus. Essentially, benefit entitlement will depend very much on your individual circumstances and what type of education you are undertaking.

****

Useful contacts

Contact a Family helpline
helpline@cafamily.org.uk
Telephone: 0808 808 3555

Independent Parental Special Education Advice (IPSEA).
IPSEA advice line
Telephone: 0800 018 4016

Student finance England 0845 300 5090 www.gov.uk/student-finance

Northern Ireland Student finance NI 0845 600 0662
www.studentfinanceni.co.uk

Scotland Student Awards Agency for Scotland 0300 555 0505
www.saas.gov.uk

Wales Student Finance Wales 0845 602 8845
www.studentfianncewales.co.uk

National Portage Association
Kings Court
17 School Road
Birmingham
B28 8JG Tel: 0121 244 1807
Fax: 0121 244 1801

www.portage.org.uk
General Enquiries info@portage.org.uk

****

Chapter 6

Help With Transport and Equipment for You and Your Disabled Child

---

You can obtain help and assistance with transport and equipment, which is designed specifically to make life easier for you and your child. Assistance with transport and equipment will also help to foster independence for your child.

This chapter outlines the main sources of transport and equipment available for you, but for more detailed advice about equipment for use inside and outside your home you should discuss this with your occupational therapist.

Welfare benefits

We covered welfare benefits in chapter 4. In addition to the various welfare benefits available to assist you with transport, there are other schemes, the most important being the schemes to help you buy a car and the Blue Badge Scheme that relates to parking for the disabled. You can also get exemption from Vehicle Road Tax.

The Blue Badge Scheme
Blue Badge parking concessions-What is the Blue Badge Scheme?

The aim of the Blue Badge scheme is to help disabled people who have severe mobility problems to access goods, services and other facilities by allowing them to park close to their destination. The scheme provides a national range of on-street parking concessions for Blue Badge holders who are travelling either as a driver or passenger.

People who automatically qualify for a badge

A person is automatically eligible for a badge if they are over two years old and meet at least one of the following criteria:

- receives the Higher Rate of the Mobility Component of the Disability Living Allowance
- is registered blind (severely sight impaired)
- receives a War Pensioner's Mobility Supplement
- has received a lump sum benefit within tariff levels 1-8 of the Armed Forces and Reserve Forces (Compensation) Scheme and has been certified as having a permanent and substantial disability which causes inability to walk or very considerable difficulty in walking

People who may also qualify for a badge

Some people may also be eligible for a badge if they are more than two years old and have a permanent and substantial disability which causes inability to walk or very considerable difficulty in walking. If you are applying for a badge under this criterion you will need to show that you/they have a permanent and substantial disability which means:

- you are unable to walk
- you are unable to walk very far without experiencing very considerable difficulty. This may include excessive pain and breathlessness, or a deterioration of health brought on by the effort needed to walk

A permanent and substantial disability is one that is likely to last for all of your life. Eligibility is not determined on the basis of a particular diagnosis or condition. It is the effect of the permanent disability on your ability to walk that is important.

You can find out more about the Blue Badge Scheme and whether you are entitled by contacting your local council.

Alternatively, you can contact the National blue badge helpline on 0844 463 0215.

The Motability Scheme

The Motability Scheme can help you with leasing a car, powered wheelchair or scooter. You'll need to be getting one of the following:

o the higher rate of the mobility component of DLA
o War Pensioners' Mobility Supplement
o the enhanced rate of the mobility component of PIP
o VAT relief for vehicles

You may not have to pay VAT on having a vehicle adapted to suit your condition, or on the lease of a Motability vehicle - this is known as VAT relief.

There are currently over 640,000 people enjoying the benefits of Motability. The following are included in the package:

- A brand new car, powered wheelchair or scooter every three years, or Wheelchair Accessible Vehicle (WAV) every five years
- Insurance, servicing and maintenance
- Full breakdown assistance
- Annual vehicle tax
- Replacement tyres (and batteries for scooters and wheelchairs)
- Windscreen repair or replacement
- 60,000 mileage allowance over three years for cars; 100,000 for WAVs
- Many adaptations at no extra cost
- Two named drivers for your car

The Motability Scheme is directed and overseen by Motability, a national charity that also raises funds and provides financial assistance to customers who would otherwise be unable to afford the mobility solution they need.

Motability Operations is a company responsible for the finance, administration and maintenance of Motability cars, scooters and powered wheelchairs.

To find out more about Motability you should contact them at the address at the end of this chapter.

Use of Public Transport

Travel permits for buses and trains

Most local authorities offer travel permits for children who are disabled and over the age of 5 years. There is normally a charge, as there is with everything and the criteria and availability of the permists will vary according to each authority, generally however, the main criteria is being in receipt of the higher rate of PIP. In some cases, your child's GP may be asked for a supporting letter. Your local council will be able to help in this regard.

Help with taxi fares

Some local councils, but not all, offer help with the cost of Black Cab taxi fares. The criteria is similar to other concessions. You should ask at your local council for details.

Community transport schemes

Many local authorities offer local community transport schemes for people with mobility problems. Again, the local authority will have details of schemes on offer in your area. There is also a national association, the Community Transport Association. The CTA is a national membership association which leads and supports community transport. Address at the end of this chapter.

Equipment available for disabled children-Equipment provision through local authorities & direct payments

Much of the equipment need by you or your child, may be provided by your local authority. This will usually occur following an assessment and recommendation by an occupational therapist and will depend on the eligibility criteria of your local authority. If your child is eligible, the equipment will be provided on a long-term loan basis. This means that the equipment will remain the property of the council, but that your child can use it for as long as they need it. The council will take responsibility for the servicing and maintenance of the equipment.

Direct payments

If your child's occupational therapy assessment shows that they need a piece of equipment but you prefer an alternative piece of equipment that meets the same need, you may be able to have a direct payment. It is now mandatory for local authorities to offer the choice of direct payments.

A direct payment is a cash payment that equals the amount it costs your local authority to supply their choice of standard equipment. You can then add your own money to this ('top-up') to buy your preferred piece of equipment. For example, your local authority may provide you with a bath lift that has a fixed angle backrest and you may wish to pay for a bath lift that has a reclining backrest. Usually you will be the joint owner of the equipment with your local authority.

Before you purchase the equipment, your local authority must be satisfied that your child's needs will be met by the item you have chosen, and that the equipment is safe. You will also need to agree with your local authority who will be responsible for the servicing and maintenance of the equipment. Following purchase, you will need to provide proof of purchase and your local authority will review the equipment to ensure safety and suitability. Note that if you receive direct payments to arrange your child's care and support at home then this must not be used to buy equipment.

Arranging an assessment

To enquire about an assessment with an occupational therapist contact your local social services. You can obtain their contact details by entering your postcode on the directgov website.

Wheelchairs

If you have a long-term or permanent difficulty with mobility, getting a wheelchair or scooter, or other mobility equipment, may help you to live more independently.

Again, you will need to consult an occupational therapist who will provide you with the advice appropriate to your specific situation. there are wheelchairs centres in each local authority area and in Scotland and Wales they are called Aritificial limb and appliance centres and in Northern Ireland they are called Prosthetic and Orthotic Aids Centres.

Other needs such as nappies and incontinence pads

If you require nappies or incontince pads, and your child is over the age of infancy, as a result of an ongoing disability, you should contact your local health authority. Your GP can advise you about what is avialble or at least point you in the right direction, as can the Health Visitor or Community Paediatrician.

Adaptations to your housing-Disabled Facilities Grants

You could get a grant from your council if your child is disabled and you need to make changes to your home, for example to widen doors and install ramps, improve access to rooms and facilities - eg stairlifts or a downstairs bathroom, provide a heating system suitable for your needs, adapt heating or lighting controls to make them easier to use.

A Disabled Facilities Grant will not affect any benefits that you're getting. How much you get depends on your household income and household savings over £6,000

Country	Grant
England	Up to £30,000
Wales	Up to £36,000
Northern Ireland	Up to £25,000
Scotland	Disabled Facilities Grants are not available - find out about support for equipment and adaptations

Depending on your income, you may need to pay towards the cost of the work to the property. Disabled children under 18 can get a grant without their parents' income being taken into account. Contact your local council for more information. You might not get any grant if you start work on your property before the council approves your application.

How and when you will be paid

You'll be paid either by instalments - as the work progresses or in full - when the work is finished. The council may pay the contractor directly, or give you a cheque to pass on - they'll agree this with you when they approve your application. You'll be paid either when the council is happy with the finished work, when you give the council the invoice, demand or receipt for payment from the contractor. Normally, if you (or a relative) does the work the council will only accept invoices for materials or services you've bought.

Eligibility

You or someone living in your property must be disabled. Either you or the person you're applying for must:

- ○ own the property or be a tenant
- ○ intend to live in the property during the grant period (which is currently 5 years)
- ○ You can also apply for a grant if you're a landlord and have a disabled tenant.

The council will needsto be happy that the work is necessary and appropriate to meet the disabled person's needs, reasonable and can be done - depending on the age and condition of the property. You might not get any grant if you start work on your property before the council approves your application.

****

Useful Contacts

Motability
www.motability.co.uk
Tel: 0300 456 4566 8am-7pm Monday to Friday 9am-1pm Saturday.

Blue badge Scheme
www.gov.uk/blue-badge-scheme-information-council
National blue badge helpline 0844 463 0215.

Community Transport Association
0345 1306195,
www.ctauk.org

Housing Ombudsman
info@housing-ombudsman.org.uk
Telephone: 0300 111 3000

Shelter England
www.shelter.org.uk
Help line 0808 800 444

Disability Housing Scotland
www.housingoptionsscotland.org.uk

Independent Living For Disabled people
www.scope.org.uk
0808 800 3333
Deals with UK housing advice for disabled

www.gov.uk/help-for-disabled-child

Chapter 7

Holidays and Breaks for Disabled Children and Their Families

Everyone, whatever their situation, needs a break from their children every now and again. Having a breathing space from caring for a disabled child is no exception. Also, your disabled child is likely to enjoy the opportunity of doing new things with other children and adults and will also probably learn much from the experience.

In addition to breaks away from your child(ren) breaks away with your child are also important and there are many organisations which can help you plan a holiday with your disabled child.

In this chapter we outline some of the possibilities for short-term breaks or respite care, such as family based schemes, play schemes or residential care, and holidays. There is also a list of organisations which may be of use to you.

Respite breaks or short term breaks

Respite care is often used to describe the situation when a child goes away from the family home overnight to give his or her parent/carer a break. In addition, respite care can also apply to care given to a child in his or her own home whilst the parent/carer goes out, and to short-term breaks during the day, such as play schemes.

Many parents find it very hard to be away from their child, even when they really need the break. This is understandable but can be overcome by planning respite care so that you and your child can get to know someone over a space of time before you leave them in charge of your child. Because respite care may be needed in an emergency - if you were taken ill, for example, and there was no one else to care for your child - is it important for you to check out the respite care possibilities at an early stage before any crisis may occur.

Different types of respite care and short-term breaks are listed and described below.

Family Based Respite Care

Family based respite care schemes are usually run by local voluntary agencies or by social services departments. They assess, recruit, train and monitor single people or families who are able to look after a disabled child in their home on a regular basis, like 1 night a fortnight, a weekend per month, or sometimes longer spells like a week or a fortnight on occasions (e.g. once/twice a year) so the parent(s) can go away.

The procedure for recruiting, assessing and approving carers is very thorough and governed by Children Act 1989 guidelines, and is very similar to the procedure for recruiting foster parents. So you can rest assured from the start that the carer matched to your child is as suitable and capable as possible.

The scheme which recruits carers for a disabled child will have information about you and your child, what the child is like, what his or her disabilities are and what his or her likes and dislikes are. They will then match you and your child with a carer they judge to be suitable for your child. They will try and match racial, cultural and religious backgrounds as far as possible. It is then usual for you and your child to meet with the prospective carer and his or her own family on several occasions, at your home and the carer's home, to get to know each other. Only after a few meetings will it be possible for your child to stay overnight at the carer's home.

Family based respite care does not always have to mean overnight care though. Many carers are willing and able to take care of children during the day during the week on occasions (during the school holidays occasionally, for example) or sometimes at the

84

weekend. This can normally be negotiated with the carer and who ever is running the scheme.

Residential Respite Care

Residential respite care units for disabled children are run by health, social services or voluntary agencies. They offer overnight care for your child on an emergency or regular basis, if you meet certain criteria which varies depending on the unit. If you are able to plan your child's first stay, it is always best to visit the unit with your child to meet the staff and look around the facilities. This will mean that parting from your child and seeing your child go away from home will be much easier for you both. You can find out about what residential respite care is available by asking your health professional, social services department or voluntary agency.

Play schemes and After School Clubs

Plays schemes for the school holidays and after school clubs are normally run by the leisure department of your local council, although some are also run by voluntary agencies. They are normally based in schools and offer play activities and outings in a relaxed but supervised environment.

Your child may be able to join the play schemes and clubs run for non-disabled children, depending on what his or her needs are. Special schemes and clubs are also run for disabled children.

Respite Care or Short-term Breaks in Your Home

There may be opportunities for respite care in your home meaning that your child can stay at home whilst you go out. This type of respite care, however, is not normally for overnights. Such breaks will usually be for care during the day, such as 2-4 hours, to give you time to go shopping, see some friends, or simply spend some time alone or with your partner. One of the main national organisations offering this type of care is the Carers Trust, which was a merger between Crossroads Caring For Carers Scheme and the princess Royal Trust for Carers. They employ carers who go into families once a week for 4 hours or twice a week for 2 hours. Most families receive a maximum of 4 hours per week but this depends on their needs and circumstances. Carers work all hours so it is possible to have help at weekends and evenings as well as during the day. Carers Trust carers work with children and people of all ages and all disabilities.

Some local Crossroads Caring for Carers schemes also offer an occasional night sitting service if your sleep is often interrupted.

Some areas may not have a Carers Trust scheme but will have a similar scheme which works under a different name. Ask the Carers Trust national organisation (address at the end of this chapter) or your local social services department, health professional or voluntary organisation to see if you have a local scheme.

Holidays

Having a disabled child should not mean that you cannot go away. There are many organisations that can help you plan a holiday with your child or who can organise an independent trip for him or her if s/he is old enough.

The numerous organisations listed overleaf publish information about holidays for the disabled including family holidays, activity holidays and holidays for unaccompanied disabled children and adults.

****

Useful Contacts

Holiday Care

0843 289 2459

www.holiday-care.co.uk

Disability Rights UK

Ground Floor

CAN Mezzanine

49-51 East Rd

London

N1 6AH

Office Number: 020 7250 8181

(this line open Mon-Fri, between 10.00 and 12.30pm and 1.30 and 4.00pm)

Disability Holidays

Registered Office:

Unit 8 Victoria Way

Newmarket

Suffolk

CB8 7SH

Email: admin@disabilityholidaysguide.com

The following organisations can provide holidays and holiday accommodation for disabled children and their families.

Break

1 Montague Road

Sheringham NR26 8LN

01263 822161

www.break-charity.org

Specialises in holidays for multiply disabled children and adults, individuals, groups and those unaccompanied by parents or staff

St Mark's Community Centre
218 Tollgate Road
Beckton
London
E6 5YA

Telephone: 01499 302715
Fax: 0207 473 7847
e-mail enquiries: contactus@across.org.uk

Organises holidays for disabled people of all ages across Europe

THE CALVERT TRUST

For all enquries relating to The Lake District Calvert Trust or general Calvert Trust questions please contact them using the details below.

Telephone: 017687 72255
Facsimile: 017687 71920
http://www.calvert-trust.org.uk/contact-us/lake-district

KESWICK
Little Crosthwaite
Keswick
Cumbria CA12 4QD
017687 72254
www.calvert-trust.keswick

EXMOOR
Wislandpound Farm

Kentisbury
North Devon EX31 4SJ
01598 763221
www.calvert-trust.org.uk/exmoor
The Calvert Trust in Northumberland, Cumbria and Devon have purpose built centres for disabled people and their families offering a wide range of sports and recreational activities.

3H Fund (Help the Handicapped Holiday Fund)
B2, Speldhurst Business Park,
Langton Road,
Speldhurst, Tunbridge Wells, Kent TN3 0AQ
Tel: 01892 860207
Email: info@3hfund.org.uk

Group holidays for physically disabled children and young people over 11 years.

National Holiday Fund For Sick and Disabled Children
NHF Office
14 Buttermere
Hemsby
Norfolk
NR29 4JZ
01493 731235

www.nhfcharity.co.uk

Provides holidays to Florida for chronically or terminally ill children and physically disabled children, between the ages of 8 and 18. Grants are not available.

FINANCING HOLIDAYS

Social Services/children's services

Disabled children and their families may be able to obtain a small grant from their social services department towards a holiday. The criteria for receiving some funding will vary from one council to another, but many means test and/or will only give money to a family every few years.

Charitable Organisations

MENCAP

The Membership Office
Mencap National Centre
123 Golden Lane
London EC1Y ORT
020 769 6900/6979
Email: holidayfund@mencap.org.uk

Provides grants towards the cost of a holiday for individuals with learning disabilities.

THE FAMILY FUND

Unit 4, Alpha Court
Monks Cross Drive
Huntington
York Y32 9WN

01904 621115
www.familyfund.org.uk
info@familyfund.org.uk

To receive funding, there must be a severely disabled child under the age of 16 in the family. Grants vary in size and can be used towards family holidays with or without the disabled child.

THE FAMILY HOLIDAY ASSOCIATION

3 Gainsford Street
London
SE1 2NE
020 3117 0650
www.familyholidayassociation.org.uk

The Family Holiday Association provides grants for families for one week's holiday of their choice. The family must be referred to the Association by social services, health professional or local voluntary organization. The child must be at least 3 years old.

PEARSON'S HOLIDAY FUND

P.O. Box 3017
South Croydon
CR2 9PN
020 8657 3053
www.pearsonsholidayfund.org.uk

Funds children aged 4-17 whilst on holiday in the U.K. The fund only deals with the referrer, i.e. the doctor, social worker, health visitor etc, rather than the family.

FAMILY WELFARE ASSOCIATION

501-505 Kingsland Road
London E8 4AU
020 7252 8283
www.fwa.org.uk

Provides grants for holidays to families with disabled children. Applications are made through social services or health professional.

Trains

Complaints and information-National Rail Enquiries Tel – 0845 748 4950. If you aren't happy with the way a train company deals with your complaint you can appeal, outside London, to: Passenger Focus (tel: 0300 123 2350).

In London-London Travel Watch at:
http://www.londontravelwatch.org.uk/ (tel: 020 3176 2999).

Air Travel

Complaints and information- Civil Aviation Authority (CAA) at the address below:

Passenger Advice and Complaints Team
4th Floor,
CAA House
45-59 Kingsway
London
WC2B 6TE

Taxi and Mini cabs

Public Carriage Office (PCO) www.pco-licence.co.uk

Specialist companies

Access Travel
www.access-travel.co.uk
Te: 01942 888844

Responsible Travel

www.responsibletravel.com Tel: 01273 823 700

Enable Holidays
0871 299 4939

Disability Travel
www.disabilitytravel.com

****

Chapter 8

Disability and Employment

Although this book is about the rights of disabled children, there might come a time, depending on the nature of your child's disability, when he or she wants to enter the workplace. This chapter covers the support and training available to help disabled people into work. It also covers employers responsibilities towards disabled people in the workplace.

Entering employment

The role of Jobcentre plus and Disability Employment Advisors

Jobcentre plus is the Department of Work and Pensions organisation providing benefits and services to people of working age. This means age 16 or over. Everyone who claims benefits from Jobcentre Plus is allocated a personal advisor to deal with claims for benefit and help them back into work. Disabled people also have access to a Disability Employment Advisor who provide employment assessment, job seeking advice and assistance with training as well as specialist advice and information. It is important to note that advice and support from a DEA is not dependant on benefits it is available to any disabled person.

Work programmes

There are a number of work programmes managed by 'providers' who are contracted by the government which aim to help people find work and stay in work. They provide activities such as work experience, work trials, help to become self-employed, voluntary work, training and ongoing support. The programmes are mandatory if a person is considered capable of work. Referral to work programmes is normally through Jobcentre Plus. If in receipt of Job Seekers Allowance a person will have to take part in the Work Programme after nine months. If the advisor agrees a person may join earlier than this if they wish. If they receive Employment and Support Allowance the time for entry to a Work Programme will vary depending on an assessment of a person's fitness to work.

Community Work Placement Programme

The Community Work Placement Programme is designed for Jobseeker's Allowance claimants who require further support to obtain and sustain employment following a Work Programme placement. Participants may have to undertake work placements for the benefit of the community and work-related activity. This programme is mandatory.

Work Choice

The work choice programme is aimed at people who are experiencing barriers to work arising from a disability or who are in work but risk losing their job as a result of a disability. Participation is voluntary and usually they must be referred by a Disability Employment Advisor. Work choice consists of three modules, each of which is tailored to their specific needs:

- o Work Entry Support-this is up to six months help with vocational guidance, confidence building, job search advice and other support such as job application skills. In some cases, this support can be for longer than six months;
- o In-Work Support-this is up to two years support once a person is in employment. The Work Choice Provider will work with them and their employer to identify the support

o needed and also help them develop the necessary skills and knowledge to move to unsupported employment;

o Longer Term In-Work Support- This is long term support offered to assist a person throughout your career.

Work choice is available throughout the UK with the exception of Northern Ireland where there are similar schemes.

Access to Work

Access to Work is designed to help disabled people overcome any barriers that they may face in obtaining employment and retaining employment. Access to Work provides practical advice and also grants towards extra costs which may be incurred arising from a disability. This advice and support can include special aids and adaptations, or equipment needed for employment, adaptations premises (not new) and equipment, help with travel, help with a support worker, a communicator and, if needed, an interpreter.

Certain types of expenditure are excluded, details of which can be obtained during the application stage. Costs which are the responsibility of the employer, for example costs which are seen as a 'reasonable adjustment' under the Equality Act 2010, are not included. (See below for details of 'reasonable adjustments').

A person will be eligible for help through the Access to Work scheme if they are employed, including as an apprentice, self-employed or unemployed and have a job to start and they are disabled. Access to Work defines disability as in the Equality Act 2010 (see introduction) but also includes impairments and health conditions that are only evident in the workplace.

Access to Work also provides help to people with mental health conditions and learning difficulties. The service provides a wide range of support for a period of six months for people with mental health conditions, including work focussed mental health support tailored to the individual, assessment of an individuals needs, a personalised support plan, advice and guidance to employers and the identification of reasonable adjustments needed in the workplace.

How much support can a person receive?

If a person has been in a job for less than six weeks, are self-employed or are about to start work, Access to Work will cover 100% of approved costs. If they have been employed for six weeks or more when they apply for help, Access to Work will pay only some of the costs of support, called 'cost sharing' which is dependant on the number of employees in an organisation. The funding agreements can last up to three years with an annual review.

For more information about Access to Work contact 020 8426 3110. Normally there will be a telephone interview by an advisor to assess eligibility. Following the phone interview the interviewee should be sent an application form (AtW1), which they should check, sign and return within a given period.

Training

There are numerous government training programmes designed to help prepare people for work. Details can be found from a nearest Jobcentre Plus office. There are many courses available designed to help disabled people. Contact a disabled employment advisor at the local Jobcentre Plus office or ring the National Careers Service Helpline 0800 100 900 or Skills Development Scotland 0800 917 8000.

Benefits while training

DLA and PIP are not usually affected if training is undertaken or if a person gets a training allowance. However, DLA care component and PIP daily living component will not usually be paid for any days that a person stays in a care home to attend a residential training programme. The residential training programmes aim to help long-term unemployed adults overcome disability related barriers to employment.

Advice concerning benefits entitlement, such as Income Support, Jobseeker's allowance and Employment and Support Allowance and how they are affected by training, can be obtained from a local Jobcentre Plus.

When a person is in work

Disability and employers responsibilities

It's against the law for employers to discriminate against anyone because of a disability. The Equality Act 2010 protects everyone and covers areas including:

- o application forms
- o interview arrangements
- o aptitude or proficiency tests
- o job offers
- o terms of employment, including pay
- o promotion, transfer and training opportunities
- o dismissal or redundancy
- o discipline and grievances

Reasonable adjustments in the workplace

Those employees with disabilities share the same employment rights as other workers with the addition of some other rights as stated within the Equality Act 2010. Within this act, employers are expected to make 'reasonable adjustments' within the workplace with regard to access and facilities for disabled members of staff. The provisions set out in the Equality Act apply to every employer, no matter the size or industry (except the armed forces). It is worth noting that the reasonable adjustment requirements are not necessary to carry out in anticipation or only in case an employer gains a disabled employee. The adjustments need only be carried out once a disabled person is employed or applies for a role within the company.

To comply with the Equality Act 2010, an employee must suffer from severe or long-term impairments. Impairments of disabled employees include:

- o Physical impairments - mobility disabilities
- o Mental impairments - long term (12 months plus) mental illnesses or learning disabilities
- o Sensory impairments - visual or hearing impairments.

What are reasonable adjustments?

The Equality Act states employers have a duty to amend the workplace in order to accommodate both disabled employees and/or applicants for job roles. These adjustments are in order to avoid disabled people being at a disadvantage when applying for a job or indeed working within an organisation. Reasonable adjustments can vary and cover areas from working arrangements to physical changes around the workplace.

Adjusted working arrangements may be flexible working hours to allow disabled employees to be able to meet their employment requirements, or amendments being made to workplace equipment, adapting it to suit employee's capabilities.

If a physical feature within the workplace creates a disadvantage for a disabled employee, steps must be taken to amend or remove the obstruction. Physical adjustments can include changes such as:

- o The addition of a ramp rather than steps to access buildings.
- o Providing disabled toilet facilities need to provided to accommodate those that need them.
- o The widening of doorways to allow for wheelchair access.

o   Repositioning door handles and/or light switches etc to ensure they can be reached.

In some cases, an employer may need to provide disabled employees with extra help through an aid to ensure that the disabled employee is not at any disadvantage against other workers. This aid may be in form of specialist or adapted equipment, such as special computer keyboards or telephones.

With regard to a disabled person applying for a job, an employer does not necessarily need to make the physical adjustments before the interview. It will suffice that an easily accessible location and necessary support and assistance for the applicant to get there is provided. If the applicant is then employed, the employer must consider the other adjustments mentioned above.

Recruitment

An employer who is recruiting staff may make limited enquiries about a person's health or disability. They can only be asked about their health or disability:

o   to help decide if they can carry out a task that is an essential part of the work
o   to help find out if they can take part in an interview
o   to help decide if the interviewers need to make reasonable adjustments for them in a selection process
o   to help monitoring
o   if they want to increase the number of disabled people they employ
o   if they need to know for the purposes of national security checks

A person may be asked whether they have a health condition or disability on an application form or in an interview. Thought needs to be given as to whether the question is one that is allowed to be asked at that stage of recruitment.

Redundancy and retirement

A person can't be chosen for redundancy just because they are disabled. The selection process for redundancy must be fair and balanced for all employees. Also, an employer cannot force a person to retire if they become disabled.

****

Useful Contacts

Access to Work 020 8426 3110.

www.evenbreak.co.uk Jobs for disabled people - Evenbreak matches disabled job seekers with employers looking to build a diverse workforce

www.gov.uk/rights-disabled-person/employment
Industrial Injuries-Barnsley Industrial Injuries Disablement Benefit centre Telephone: 0345 758 5433

National Careers Service Helpline 0800 100 900 or Skills Development Scotland 0800 917 8000.

****

Index

****

Appendix 1

Welfare benefits generally

As pointed out in this book, only certain benefits may be relevant to a parent of a disabled child. These have been outlined in chapter 3. However, as a reference point the following overview of all benefits available to people, whether parents of a disabled child or not, should prove useful. The following benefits are outlined:

- ➢ Attendance Allowance
- ➢ Personal Independence Payment
- ➢ Carers Allowance
- ➢ Housing Benefit
- ➢ Council Tax Support
- ➢ Pension Credit
- ➢ Income Support
- ➢ Job Seekers Allowance
- ➢ Employment and Support Allowance
- ➢ Universal Credit
- ➢ Tax Credits
- ➢ Winter Fuel payment
- ➢ Cold weather Payment
- ➢ TV Licence Concessions
- ➢ Bereavement Allowance

Attendance Allowance

You should be able to claim Attendance Allowance if your ability to look after your own personal care is affected by physical or mental illness or disability. Attendance Allowance has 2 weekly rates, and the rate you get very much depends on the help you need. The current rates are:

- £55.10 if you need help in the day or at night

111

- £82.30 if you need help both in the day and at night.

Claiming Attendance Allowance won't affect any other income you receive, and it's also tax-free. If you are awarded it, you may become entitled to other benefits, such as Pension Credit, Housing Benefit or Council Tax Reduction, or an increase in these benefits.

You may be eligible for Attendance Allowance if you are 65 or over (if you're under 65, you may be eligible for Personal Independence Payment instead-see below), could benefit from help with personal care, such as getting washed or dressed, or supervision to keep you safe during the day or night, have any type of disability or illness, including sight or hearing impairments, or mental health issues such as dementia and have needed help for at least 6 months. (If you're terminally ill you can make a claim straight away.)

Attendance Allowance isn't means-tested, so your income and savings aren't taken into account. You don't actually have to receive help from a carer, as Attendance Allowance is based on the help you need, not the help you actually get. Also, you don't strictly have to spend your Attendance Allowance on care – it's up to you how you use it. You can get a claim form by calling the Attendance Allowance helpline on 0845 605 6055 or 0345 605 6055 (textphone: 0845 604 5312). You can also download a claim form or claim online.

Attendance Allowance doesn't usually take into account problems with housework, cooking, shopping and gardening. If your application is turned down, ask an advice agency such as Citizens Advice about whether you should challenge the decision. Many applications are turned down because people don't mention or aren't clear about how their illness or disability affects their lives.

Personal Independence Payment

Personal Independence Payment (PIP) is a benefit for people of working age with disabilities. It has replaced Disability Living

Allowance (DLA) for anyone making a new claim. If you're under 65 and already claiming DLA you'll eventually be asked to claim PIP instead. If you were 65 or over on 8 April 2013 and already claiming DLA, you won't be affected by the change and you'll continue to get DLA payments for as long as you're entitled to them.

You may be eligible for PIP if you're under 65 and need help with daily living activities or help getting around, or both. If you are 65 or over and you have care needs, you can't claim PIP but you may be able to claim Attendance Allowance. If you are awarded PIP before you are 65 it can continue after age 65. PIP isn't based on National Insurance contributions and isn't means-tested. You can claim it whether you're working or not.

Rates of Personal Independence Payment

PIP has two parts – a **daily living component** and a **mobility component.** They're paid at different rates, depending on the level of difficulty you have performing particular activities such as preparing food and drink or dressing and undressing. You may be able to claim one or both components.

Daily living component:

Standard rate - £55.10 per week
Enhanced rate - £82.30 per week

Mobility component:

Standard rate - £21.80 per week
Enhanced rate - £57.45 per week

To start your claim you'll need to call the Department for Work and Pensions (DWP) on 0800 917 2222 (textphone 0800 917

777). They will ask you for basic information and then send you a claim form. Most people will have to attend a face-to-face assessment of their needs as well. Find out more on the Gov.UK website. If your application is turned down contact an advice agency such as Citizens Advice about whether you should challenge the decision. Your needs may change and increase, so even if you're not eligible for PIP now, you may be able to claim successfully in the future.

Carer's Allowance

The main welfare benefit for carers is called Carer's Allowance and it's worth £62.10 per week if you're eligible. You don't have to be related to or live with the person you care for to claim Carer's Allowance. You'll also get National Insurance credits each week towards your pension if you're under pension age.

You may not think of yourself as a carer. Perhaps you've looked after someone for a long time without ever calling yourself one, or maybe you think the help you give your spouse or parent is simply what you should be doing. If so, you may have been missing out on the help that is available to you.

To claim Carer's Allowance, you must:

- spend at least 35 hours a week caring for a disabled person - you don't have to live with them
- care for someone who receives the higher- or middle-rate care component of Disability Living Allowance, either rate of Personal Independence Payment daily living component, or any rate of Attendance Allowance
- not earn more than £102 a week (after deductions)
- not be in full-time education.

Carer's Allowance may not be paid if you're receiving a State Pension or certain other benefits, but it's still worth claiming because you could get extra Pension Credit and/or Housing Benefit.

If you're claiming Universal Credit You may be able to get an extra amount because of your caring role without having to apply for Carer's Allowance. (see below for universal credit).

If you want to make a claim for carers allowance call the Carer's Allowance Unit on 0845 608 4321 (textphone: 0845 604 5312) to request a claim pack. Or you can visit GOV.UK to download a claim form or make a claim online.

Housing Benefit

Housing Benefit helps pay your rent if you are a tenant on a low income. It will not only reduce your rent but also cover some service charges like lifts and communal laundry facilities. How much you get depends on a number of factors:

- if you rent privately or from a council
- your household income and circumstances
- if you have empty rooms

You may receive more Housing Benefit if you get a disability or carer's benefit, such as Carer's Allowance, Attendance Allowance or Personal Independence Payment.

Housing Benefit is a means-tested benefit. The amount you can claim is affected by: your savings, who you live with, how much rent you pay and how many rooms you have in your home. If you get the Guarantee Credit part of Pension Credit you may get your rent paid in full by Housing Benefit. If you don't get Guarantee Credit - but have a low income and less than £16,000 in savings - you may still get some help.

You can't claim Housing Benefit if you own your own home. However, you may be eligible for Support with Mortgage Interest as part of Pension. If you're not claiming other benefits, you can get a claim form from your local council. You can apply for Housing

Benefit at the same time as applying for Pension Credit. If you're already claiming Pension Credit, contact the Pension Service.

Council Tax Support

You may be eligible for Council Tax Support if you're on a low income or claim certain benefits. Council Tax Support replaced Council Tax Benefit in 2013, and each local authority now runs their own Council Tax Support schemes. Apply directly to your local council to see if you're entitled to support.

The support you get may depend on factors such as which benefits you receive, your age, your income, savings, who you live with and how much Council Tax you pay. If you receive a disability or carer's benefit, you may get more Council Tax Support. You may even get your Council Tax paid in full if you get the Guarantee Credit part of Pension Credit. If you don't get Guarantee Credit but have a low income and less than £16,000 in savings, you may still get some help. You can apply whether you own your home, rent, are working or currently unemployed.

Universal Credit

If you're of working age and making a new claim in an area where Universal Credit has been introduced, you should claim Universal Credit to help with your rent. See below for more about Universal Credit.

Pension Credit

Pension Credit is an income-related benefit that comes in two parts and you may be eligible for one or both:

- Guarantee Credit tops up your weekly income to a guaranteed minimum level
- Savings Credit is extra money if you've got some savings or your income is higher than the basic State Pension

About 4 million older people are entitled to Pension Credit, yet about 1 in 3 of those eligible are still not claiming it. Don't be put off if you discover you're only eligible for a small amount of Pension Credit. It's your passport to other benefits, such as Housing Benefit and Council Tax Reduction.

Rates of Pension Credit
Guarantee Credit will top up your weekly income to:

- £151.20 if you're single
- or £230.85 if you're a couple.

If you qualify for Savings Credit, you can get up to:

- £14.82 extra per week if you're single
- or £17.43 if you're a couple.

Claiming Guarantee Credit
The minimum age to claim Guarantee Credit is gradually rising. In April 2015, it's 62 and a half years. If your weekly income is less than £151.20 if you're single, or £230.80 if you're a couple you may qualify for Guarantee Credit. If you have a disability, are a carer or have to pay housing costs, you may be eligible even if your income is higher than the amounts given above.

Claiming Savings Credit
If you're 65 or over you may also qualify for Savings Credit. There isn't a savings limit for Pension Credit, but if you have over £10,000 this will affect the amount you receive. Remember, you can claim one or both parts of Pension Credit.

Benefits of claiming Pension Credit

Pension Credit is also your passport to lots of other savings such as:

- It's unlikely you'll have to pay Council Tax (unless other people live with you).
- You'll get free NHS dental treatment, and you can claim help towards the cost of glasses and travel to hospital.
- You'll get a Cold Weather Payment of £25 when the temperature is 0°C or below for 7 days in a row.
- If you rent your home, you may get your rent paid in full by Housing Benefit.
- If you own your home, you may be eligible for help with mortgage interest, ground rent and service charges.
- If you're a carer, you may get an extra amount known as Carer Premium, or Carer Addition if it's paid with Pension Credit. This is worth up to £34.60 a week.

How make the claim

Call the Pension Credit claim line on 0800 99 1234 (textphone: 0800 169 0133).

Income Support

Income Support is a benefit for people under Pension Credit qualifying age and living on a low income. If you can't work for whatever reason or don't work many hours, you may get some support to top up your income. You can claim Income Support if you're all of the following:

- below the age you can claim Pension Credit
- a carer or, in some cases, if you're sick or disabled, or a single parent with a child under 5
- on a low income and have less than £16,000 in savings

118

- working fewer than 16 hours a week (if you have a partner they must work fewer than 24 hours a week).

If you qualify for Income Support, you could be entitled to other benefits, such as Housing Benefit or help with Council Tax, health costs or urgent one-off expenses.

Rates of Income support

- £73.10 a week if you're single
- £114.85 a week if you're a couple.

The amount you get may vary depending on your circumstances. For example you may get extra if you're a pensioner or if you're disabled. You can claim Income Support by phone. Contact Jobcentre Plus on 0800 055 6688 or textphone 0800 023 4888. Or you can you can fill out a claim form on GOV.UK. Print it out and post it to your local Jobcentre.

Jobseeker's Allowance

Jobseeker's Allowance is a taxable benefit to support people who are actively looking for work. To get Jobseeker's Allowance you must be either unemployed or working fewer than 16 hours a week.

If you're a couple and both out of work, you may have to make a joint claim. There are 2 types of Jobseeker's Allowance:

- Contribution-based Jobseeker's Allowance pays £73.10 a week.

You can get this if you've paid enough National Insurance contributions over the last 2 years. It's paid for up to 6 months. You may get less if you have income from a part-time job or a private pension.

- Income-based Jobseeker's Allowance pays £73.10 a week if you're single and £114.85 a week if you're a couple.

The amount of income-based Jobseeker's Allowance you get may vary according to your age and whether you get disability or carer's benefits. It's means-tested so the amount you get will be affected by your savings. You can't get income-based Jobseeker's Allowance if you have over £16,000 in savings or if you or your partner works 24 or more hours a week.

To make a claim for Jobseeker's Allowance, contact your local Jobcentre Plus on 0800 055 6688 (textphone 0800 023 4888). You can also make a claim online on GOV.UK. When you make a claim, a Jobcentre Plus personal adviser will write out a Jobseeker's Agreement with you setting out the type of work you want and the steps you'll take to find a job. If your adviser feels you're not keeping to this agreement or if you pull out of a compulsory employment scheme, you can be sanctioned. This means your benefits could be reduced or stopped for a period.

Employment and Support Allowance

Employment and Support Allowance (ESA) is a benefit for people who are unable to work due to illness or disability. There are 2 types of ESA, and you may be entitled to one or both of them:

- Contribution-based ESA - you can get this if you've paid enough National Insurance contributions. It's taxable.
- Income-related ESA - you can get this if you have no income or a low income. You don't have to have paid National Insurance contributions and it isn't taxable.

During your claim you'll be called to 2 compulsory reviews, one after 13 weeks and the other after 26 weeks. You can't claim income-related ESA if you claim Universal Credit or have savings of more than £16,000.

You'll have to attend a medical assessment called a 'work capability assessment'. You'll also have to fill in a 'limited capacity for work' questionnaire that looks at how your illness or disability affects what you do. After this you'll be told whether you're considered fit for work, or whether you're entitled to ESA.

If you are entitled to ESA, you'll be placed in the 'work-related activity group' or the 'support group'. People in the support group are exempt from the benefit cap. People in the work-related activity group get less money and are expected to prepare for an eventual return to the job market. If you don't, your benefit can be reduced for a period.

If you're entitled to income-related ESA, you may also qualify for other benefits such as Housing Benefit, Council Tax Reduction and help with health costs.

Rates of ESA
Income-related ESA

The amount of you get depends on your income and savings, whether you're single or a couple, whether you get disability or carer's benefits, and the result of your assessment. Income-related ESA can be paid on its own or as a top-up to contribution-based ESA.

Contribution-based ESA

You'll get a basic allowance of £73.10 for the first 13 weeks. After your assessment, you'll get: up to £102.15 a week if you're in the work-related activity group or up to £109.30 a week if you're in the support group. If you're in the work-related activity group, you'll get contribution-based ESA for one year; if you're in the support group, there's no time limit. Contribution-based ESA may be reduced if you have a private pension or you're claiming certain benefits.

To claim call Jobcentre Plus on 0800 055 6688 (textphone 0800 023 4888). They'll ask you questions over the phone and fill in the form for you. Or visit the GOV.UK website to download a claim form. Some benefits are means-tested. In other words, the amount of income and capital you have can affect your eligibility. Capital includes savings, investments, and property other than your own home.

Different means-testing rules apply, depending on whether you're under or over the minimum State Pension age. The information on this page only applies to people over the current minimum State Pension age (rising from 60 to 66 between 2010 and 2020). This information may also not apply to couples with one person under and the other over the minimum State Pension age.

Universal Credit

Universal Credit is a new benefit gradually being introduced nationally. It will eventually replace existing benefits:

- Income-based Jobseeker's Allowance
- Income-related Employment and Support Allowance
- Income Support
- Working Tax Credit
- Child Tax Credit
- Housing Benefit.

Who can get Universal Credit?

Universal Credit is gradually being rolled out across the UK, and it may not yet be available in the area where you live. To find out when Universal Credit will be rolled out in your area, contact Jobcentre Plus on 0800 055 6688 (textphone 0800 023 4888) or visit GOV.UK.

You may be able to claim Universal Credit if you're out of work or on a low income. If you qualify for other benefits such as contribution-based Jobseeker's Allowance or contribution-based Employment and Support Allowance, you should claim them as well as Universal Credit.

The amount of Universal Credit you get will depend on a number of factors, such as the amount of hours you work or how much savings you have. You can't get Universal Credit if you have savings of more than £16,000. Standard Universal Credit payments are:

- £317.82 per month if you're single
- £498.89 per month if you're a couple

You may be entitled to extra amounts if you have housing costs, caring responsibilities, dependent children

Claiming Universal Credit

You have to fill out an online claim form on GOV.UK. If you need help filling out the form, call the Universal Credit helpline on 0845 600 0723 (or textphone 0845 600 0743).Your online claim will be followed by a face-to-face interview.

When you make a claim you will have to agree to certain conditions in return for your benefit. This may be carrying out a training course, or agreeing to the number of hours you'll spend looking for work each week. This could be the case even if you're currently unable to work due to illness. If you don't meet the conditions, your benefit may be reduced.

Caps on all benefits

The government has imposed a cap on the amount of benfits an inividual or couple/family can receive over the course of a year. The cap applies to the total amount that the people in your household get from the following benefits:

- Bereavement Allowance
- Carer's Allowance
- Child Benefit
- Child Tax Credit
- Employment and Support Allowance (unless you get the support component)
- Guardian's Allowance
- Housing Benefit
- Incapacity Benefit
- Income Support
- Jobseeker's Allowance
- Maternity Allowance
- Severe Disablement Allowance
- Widowed Parent's Allowance (or Widowed Mother's Allowance or Widows Pension you started getting before 9 April 2001)

The level of the cap is:

- £500 a week for couples (with or without children living with them)
- £500 a week for single parents whose children live with them
- £350 a week for single adults who don't have children, or whose children don't live with them

This may mean the amount you get for certain benefits will go down to make sure that the total amount you get isn't more than the cap level.

Who won't be affected?

You might still be affected by the cap if you have any grown-up children or non-dependants who live with you and they qualify for one of the benefits below. This is because they won't normally count as part of your household.

You're not affected by the benefit cap if anyone in your household qualifies for Working Tax Credit or gets any of the following benefits:

- Disability Living Allowance
- Personal Independence Payment
- Attendance Allowance
- Industrial Injuries Benefits (and equivalent payments as part of a war disablement pension or the Armed Forces Compensation Scheme)
- Employment and support allowance if you get the support component
- War Widow's or War Widower's Pension
- War pensions
- Armed Forces Compensation Scheme
- Armed Forces Independence Payment

Tax credits

Working Tax Credit

You can get Working Tax Credit if you or your partner are working enough hours a week and your income is low enough. You don't need to have children to qualify. You must be living in the UK.

The number of hours a week you have to work to be able to get Working Tax Credit depends on your circumstances. If you're single or in a couple, and have no children, you can qualify if: you are 25 or over and you work at least 30 hours a week, or you are 16 or over and you work at least 16 hours a week and you are disabled and you get a qualifying benefit, or you are 60 or over and you work at least 16 hours a week.

If you're single and have at least one child, you can qualify if you are 16 or over and you work at least 16 hours a week and you are responsible for a child or young person.

Working Tax Credits and children

If you are responsible for a child or young person, you can get Working Tax Credit provided you work at least 16 hours a week if you're single, or at least 24 hours between you if you're in a couple, with one of you working at least 16 hours a week. Some couples with children may qualify without working for 24 hours between them, provided one of them works 16 hours. Your income also needs to be low enough. A child is someone under 16, and a young person is someone who is 16, 17, 18 or 19 and still in full-time education up to A level or equivalent, or on certain approved training courses. You are responsible for a child or young person if they normally live with you or you have main responsibility for their care. You cannot usually get Working Tax Credit if your child is in local authority care.

You may be able to get Working Tax Credit for a short period after your child is 16 or leaves school, depending on when their birthday is and what they do on leaving school.

If you are on maternity leave, paternity leave or adoption leave and you normally work 16 hours or more, you can claim Working Tax Credit before you go back to work, as long as you are responsible for a child. If it is your first baby and you are not responsible for any other children, you will have to wait until the child is born, or comes to live with you before you can claim.

Working Tax Credit and disability

You can get Working Tax Credit if you are disabled provided you work at least 16 hours a week and your income is low enough and you get certain benefits because of your disability and your disability puts you at a disadvantage in getting a job.

The qualifying benefits include Incapacity Benefit, Disability Living Allowance, Personal Independence Payment, Armed Forces Independence Payment, Employment and Support Allowance, Attendance Allowance, Industrial Injuries Disablement Benefit, Statutory Sick Pay, a war pension with constant attendance allowance, occupational sick pay or Income Support or National Insurance credits awarded because you have been unable to work. There are rules about how long you have to have been getting some of these benefits before you claim Working Tax Credit. Some of these benefits stop once you are working, and some carry on.

Income levels and Working Tax Credits
Even if you meet the work conditions, you will only get Working Tax Credit if you have a low enough income. Your income for tax credits is assessed on an annual basis. Whether or not you get Working Tax Credit, and how much you get, depends on your income and your circumstances. Not all your income will be taken into account (for example, maintenance and child support, most Statutory Maternity, Paternity or Adoption Pay and all Maternity Allowance paid to you is ignored). Usually, HM Revenue and Customs (HMRC) will use your income for the previous tax year to work out what you are due.

Working Tax Credit rates
The maximum Working Tax Credit you can get is calculated by adding together different elements which are based on your circumstances. There is a basic element which is included for anyone who is entitled to Working Tax Credit. There is a second adult element if you are claiming as a member of a couple although there are some circumstances where a couple will not get this. You have to claim as a couple if you live with a partner. This includes a

partner of the opposite or same sex. There is a lone parent element if you are a lone parent.

There is a 30 hour element if you work at least 30 hours a week (or if you are claiming as a couple with a child and you jointly work at least 30 hours). There is a disability element if you are disabled, get certain benefits and you work at least 16 hours a week. You can also get a disability element if your partner qualifies for it or two disability elements if you both qualify.

There is a severe disability element if you get the highest rate care component of Disability Living Allowance, the enhanced rate of the daily living component of Personal Independence Payment, the higher rate of Attendance Allowance, or Armed Forces Independence Payment. You will get two severe disability elements if you and your partner both qualify.

You may also be able to get a childcare element. This is equivalent to up to 70% of childcare costs provided by a registered childminder, out-of-school club or another approved provider. There is a limit on the maximum eligible weekly childcare cost which means that the most this element can be is 70% of the maximum.

Rates of Working Tax Credit

Element of Working Tax Credit	Maximum annual amount from 6 April 2014	Maximum annual amount from 6 April 2015
Basic element	£1,940	£1,960
Second adult element	£1,990	£2,010
Lone parent element	£1,990	£2,010
30 hour element	£800	£810
Disability element	£2,935	£2,970
Severe disability element	£1,255	£1,275
Childcare element (up to 70% of the maximum):	Maximum weekly amount from 6 April	Maximum weekly amount from 6 April

Element of Working Tax Credit	Maximum annual amount from 6 April 2014	Maximum annual amount from 6 April 2015
	2014	2015
Maximum weekly eligible cost for one child	£175 (maximum payable £122)	£175 (maximum payable £122)
Maximum weekly eligible cost for two or more children	£300 (maximum payable £210)	£300 (maximum payable £210)

Calculating Working Tax Credit

To work out how much Working Tax Credit is due, the separate elements of Working Tax Credit which apply to you are added together. If you are entitled to Child Tax Credit as well as Working Tax Credit, your maximum Child Tax Credit is worked out at the same time and added to your maximum Working Tax Credit.

Your income for the tax year is compared to a threshold of £6,420. Usually, your income for the previous tax year is used. If your income is less than the threshold, you get the maximum Working Tax Credit (and Child Tax Credit if this applies). If your income is more than the threshold, your tax credit will be reduced. Working Tax Credit (except for the childcare element) is taken away first, followed by the childcare element. If your income is too high, you will not get any Working Tax Credit. However, you may still get some Child Tax Credit, if you are entitled, because this is the last part of your total tax credits to be reduced.

To apply for Working Tax Credit, contact the Tax Credit helpline for an application pack. The application form for your first claim is Form TC600. The helpline number is 0345 300 3900 (textphone 0345 300 3909).

When you apply for Working Tax Credit, you will have to provide your national insurance number. You will normally also have to give the national insurance number of any partner who lives with you. If you don't know your national insurance number, but you think you have one, try to provide information that will help the office find your number. If you do not have a national insurance number, you will have to apply for one.

You may be able to get some Working Tax Credit for a period before you apply, if you met the conditions and could have claimed earlier. You can normally only get Working Tax Credit backdated for a maximum of 31 days before the date you apply.

How is Working Tax Credit paid?

Working Tax Credit can be paid directly into your bank or building society account, or into a post office card account. If you do not give your account details to HM Revenue and Customs (HMRC), you may lose your entitlement to Working Tax Credit. If you have difficulties opening an account, you should get in touch with HMRC and explain.

Tax credits are awarded for a complete tax year. A tax year runs from 6 April one year to 5 April the next year. If you claim after April, your award will run from the date you claim to the end of the tax year. The amount you get is usually set for a year. If your circumstances change during the period of your award you should tell HMRC as soon as possible. This is important because otherwise you may not be paid all the tax credit you are entitled to or you may be paid too much and have to pay it back to HMRC. Some changes to your circumstances mean that your award ends and you have to claim again. Other changes mean that your award continues but it will be recalculated, and some will not affect your current award at all.

Shortly after the end of the tax year, HMRC will send you an annual review pack which may ask you to give them further information. They call this a renewal pack. However, it's very important that you provide any information requested, even if you don't want to renew your claim, because HMRC will use this to finalise your award for the year just ended. If you don't reply when asked to do so, your payments will stop and you may have to pay back an overpayment.

If your work ends, you can carry on getting Working Tax Credit for a further four weeks. This also applies if you start to work less than 16 hours a week, or in some cases, less than 30 hours a week.

If you are refused Working Tax Credit and think you are entitled, or that the amount you are awarded is wrong, call the Tax Credits Helpline and ask HM Revenue and Customs (HMRC) to explain their decision. If you are not satisfied with the explanation, you can make a formal request for the decision to be looked at again. This is called a mandatory reconsideration. You must ask for a reconsideration within 30 days of the date of the decision. If you are not satisfied with the result of the reconsideration, you can then appeal to an independent tribunal.

It's against the law for you to be treated unfairly because of your race, sex, disability, sexuality, religion or belief when HMRC decide about your Working Tax Credit claim. Also, HMRC has a policy which says they will not discriminate against you because of other things, such as if you've got HIV or if you have caring responsibilities. If you feel that you've been discriminated against, you can make a complaint about this.

Other help when you get Working Tax Credit

When you get Working Tax Credit, you may be entitled to other financial help. If you pay rent, you may be able to get Housing Benefit. If you have to pay Council Tax, you may be able to get Council Tax Reduction. Being on Working Tax Credit may also give you access to other help. For example, you may be entitled to health benefits, including free prescriptions. You may also be able get help with the costs of a new baby from a Sure Start maternity grant or help with the costs of a funeral from a funeral payment. Whether or not you can get this help will depend on your income, whether you get a disability element with your Working Tax Credit and whether you also get Child Tax Credit.

Winter Fuel Payment

Winter Fuel Payment or Winter Fuel Allowance is an annual payment to help with heating costs, made to households with someone over Pension Credit age. Not heating homes properly puts people at risk of cold-related illnesses such as a heart attack or even hypothermia. The rates for winter fuel payment currently are £200 if you're under 80 and £300 if you're 80 or over

In winter 2015-16, you will qualify for the payment if you were born before 5 January 1953.

You only need to claim once. After this, you should get it automatically each year, as long as your circumstances do not change. The payment is made directly into your bank account in November or December. For more information you should call the Winter Fuel Payments Helpline on 0845 915 1515.

Cold Weather Payment

Cold Weather Payments are made to eligible people when the weather is very cold. You get £25 a week when the average temperature has been, or is expected to be, 0°C or below for 7 days in a row (between 1 November and 31 March).

You automatically receive the payment, if you get Pension Credit or certain other means-tested benefits. If you think that you are entitled to a cold weather payment and don't get one contact the Pension Service.

TV licence concessions

You could be entitled to a concession for a TV licence if you are over 75 or someone who is over 75 lives with you. You could also be entitled if you are registered as blind or severely sight impaired or are retired or disabled and live in certain accommodation

The TV licence for your main home doesn't cover you if you have a second home. You will have to buy a separate licence. If you have a licence for your main home, you won't need another if you have a static caravan or mobile home and you don't use the TV at the same time in both places.

You need to apply for a free TV licence if you're 75 or over as it's not given out automatically. You'll need to provide your date of birth and National insurance number (or a photocopy of your passport, driving licence or birth certificate). If you share your house with someone younger than 75, you can still apply for a free licence but it must be in your name. You can apply for your concession by calling 0300 790 6165 or visiting the TV licensing website. Once you have your free TV licence, it will renew automatically annually.

If you apply for a TV licence and you are 74 when you renew your licence you can apply for a short term licence until you are 75.

Concessions for blind and sight-impaired

If you're blind or severely sight-impaired, you can claim a 50% discount on your TV licence. When you apply, you'll need to provide a photocopy of the certificate from your local authority or ophthalmologist confirming your status as well as your TV licence application form and fee. Once you're registered, all your TV licence renewals will be at the concessionary rate.

If you live with someone who is blind or severely-sight impaired, you can get the 50% discount if you transfer the TV licence to the name of that person. You can apply for your concession by calling 0300 790 6165 or visiting the TV licensing website. If you've already paid the TV licence fee but qualify for the blind concession, fill out the TV Licensing online refund form.

Care homes and sheltered housing

You may be entitled to a TV licence concession if you live in a care home or sheltered housing. This licence is called an

Accommodation for Residential Care (ARC) licence and it costs £7.50. You'll only need to get one if you watch TV in your own separate accommodation, not if you only watch it in common areas such as a residents' lounge. To qualify, you must be retired and aged 60 or over or disabled and live in accommodation which is eligible. If you think you qualify, contact the warden, staff or managing authority where you live. They will apply for one for you.

If you've already paid your full licence fee and now qualify for an ARC licence, ask your care home manager to help you apply for a refund. If you have questions about the ARC licence, phone TV licensing on 0300 790 6011 or visit the TV licensing website.

Bereavement allowance

Bereavement benefits include:

- o Bereavement Payment - a one-off lump sum you claim when your spouse or civil partner dies
- o Widowed Parent's Allowance if you have dependent Bereavement Allowance if you don't have dependent children

Bereavement benefits are paid to widows, widowers or the surviving partner of a civil partnership. You can get a bereavement benefit if your husband, wife or civil partner died on or after 9 April 2001. If you are a man whose wife died before this date, you may still be able to get some benefit.

You can get a bereavement benefit if you were legally married to your husband or wife who has now died. You can also get a bereavement benefit if you and your same-sex partner who has died registered a civil partnership.

You can't get any of the bereavement benefits if you were divorced from your husband or wife when they died, or you and your civil partner had dissolved your civil partnership. You are also excluded from claiming bereavement benefits if you remarry, or register another civil partnership. If you are getting a bereavement benefit when you remarry or register another civil partnership, it will stop. Even if you do not remarry or register another civil partnership, you cannot get bereavement benefits if you live with another partner. You can't get bereavement benefits in prison.

Bereavement Payment

A Bereavement Payment is a one-off tax-free lump sum payment of £2,000. You can claim it if you were widowed on or after 9 April 2001. You must claim within twelve months of your husband's, wife's or civil partner's death, unless there are exceptional circumstances which mean that you did not know about the death or it was not confirmed.

You are entitled to a Bereavement Payment if your husband, wife, or civil partner who has died paid enough national insurance contributions. If they died as the result of an industrial accident or an industrial disease, it does not matter whether they paid enough contributions or not.

To get Bereavement Payment you must have been below state pension age when your husband, wife or civil partner died, or - if you were over state pension age - they must not have been entitled to state retirement pension, based on their own national insurance contributions, when they died. You must have been married to your husband or wife, or in a registered civil partnership with your partner when they died. Until 6 April 2010, state pension age was 60 for a woman and 65 for a man. Since this date, the minimum age at which both men and women can claim a state pension is gradually being set to age 65 and will be increased, depending on which year you were born.

In England and Wales, you can claim a Bereavement Payment and tell the DWP about the death at the same time, by calling the DWP Bereavement Service on:

Telephone: 0845 606 0265
Textphone: 0845 606 0285
Telephone: 0845 606 0275 (Welsh)
Textphone: 0845 606 0295 (Welsh)

The Bereavement Service can take your claim for bereavement benefits over the phone and do a benefits check to see if you qualify for any other benefits as a result of the death.

Widowed Parent's Allowance

Widowed Parent's Allowance is a weekly payment made to a widow, widower or surviving civil partner with dependent children. Your husband, wife or civil partner must usually have died on or after 9 April 2001. However, if you are a man and your wife died before this date, you were under 65 when she died and you did not re-marry before 9 April 2001, you can also claim Widowed Parent's Allowance.

You can get Widowed Parent's Allowance if you are bringing up a child or you are a woman expecting your husband's baby. You can also get Widowed Parent's Allowance if you are a woman who was living with your civil partner when she died and you are pregnant as a result of fertility treatment.

If you are bringing up a child you must usually be getting Child Benefit for that child. The child should be:

o the child of you and your late spouse, or
o the child of you and your late civil partner, or
o a child who you or your late spouse or civil partner got Child Benefit for at the time of your spouse or civil partner's death (for example, it could be your adopted child or a step-child).

You must have been under state pension age when your husband, wife or civil partner died, and your spouse or civil partner must have paid enough national insurance contributions for you to get Widowed Parent's Allowance. The only exception is if their death was caused by an industrial injury or an industrial disease, when it does not matter if enough national insurance contributions had been paid. If you need more information about the contribution conditions for Widowed Parent's Allowance, you should consult an experienced adviser, for example, at a Citizens Advice Bureau.

The amount of the basic Widowed Parent's Allowance will depend on your late husband, wife or civil partner's national insurance contributions, unless they died because of an industrial injury or disease.

In England and Wales, you can report the death and claim Widowed Parent's Allowance by calling the Department for Work and Pensions (DWP) Bereavement Service. They will take a claim for bereavement benefits over the phone. In Northern Ireland, call the Social Security Agency Bereavement Service.

In the same phone call, the DWP can also do a benefits check to see if you qualify for any other benefits as a result of the death. Alternatively, you can claim Widowed Parent's Allowance on form BB1. You can get form BB1 from your local Jobcentre Plus office or, in England, Wales and Scotland, from the GOV.UK website at www.gov.uk or by calling Jobcentre Plus on:

Freephone: 0800 055 6688
Textphone: 0800 023 4888
Welsh language line: 0800 012 1888

You should claim Widowed Parent's Allowance within three months of the date of death, to avoid losing any money. If you claim later than this, your benefit can only be backdated for up to three months

If you claim late, you can ask for backdating on the claim form. You do not have to give a reason for claiming late as long as you can show that you were entitled to Widowed Parent's Allowance before you made your claim. In some cases, you may be able to get Widowed Parent's Allowance for more than three months before you made your claim.

You can get Widowed Parent's Allowance until you stop getting Child Benefit. If this happens within 52 weeks of your husband, wife or civil partner's death, you can claim Bereavement Allowance for the rest of the 52 weeks.

Widow's pension

Widow's Pension is paid until you are 65, when you become entitled to a Retirement Pension at the same rate as the Widow's Pension. If you are over state pension age (60) but under 65, you can choose to stay on Widow's Pension or claim Retirement Pension.

Payments for funeral expenses

If you have to pay for a funeral for your partner, a close relative or friend, you may be able to claim a funeral payment from the Social Fund. Partners include lesbian, gay and heterosexual partners, whether you were married, in a civil partnership or living together. To get a funeral payment, you must be getting Income Support, income-based Jobseeker's Allowance, income-related Employment and Support Allowance, Pension Credit, Universal Credit or Housing Benefit. Some people getting Child Tax Credit or Working Tax Credit may also be entitled to a funeral payment.

Financial help if your husband, wife or civil partner was in the Armed Forces

If your husband, wife or civil partner died as a result of serving in the Armed Forces, you may be able to get financial help from the

Service Personnel and Veterans Agency (SPVA). It does not matter whether your husband, wife or civil partner died during active service or not, as long as the death was caused by service in the Armed Forces. You may get a War Widow's or War Widower's pension, or a guaranteed income payment (based on your spouse or civil partner's earnings), depending on when the injury, illness or death was caused.

****

www.straightforwardco.co.uk

All titles, listed below, in the Straightforward Guides Series can be purchased online, using credit card or other forms of payment by going to www.straightfowardco.co.uk A discount of 25% per title is offered with online purchases.

Law
A Straightforward Guide to:

Consumer Rights
Bankruptcy Insolvency and the Law
Employment Law
Private Tenants Rights
Family law
Small Claims in the County Court
Contract law
Intellectual Property and the law
Divorce and the law
Leaseholders Rights
The Process of Conveyancing
Knowing Your Rights and Using the Courts
Producing Your own Will
Housing Rights
The Bailiff the law and You
Probate and The Law
Company law
What to Expect When You Go to Court
Give me Your Money-Guide to Effective Debt Collection
Rights of Disabled people

General titles
Letting Property for Profit

Buying, Selling and Renting property
Buying a Home in England and France
Buying and Selling a Property Abroad
Bookkeeping and Accounts for Small Business
Creative Writing
Freelance Writing
Writing Your own Life Story
Writing Performance Poetry
Writing Romantic Fiction
Essay Writing
Speech Writing
Teaching Your Child to Read and write
Creating a Successful Commercial Website
The Straightforward Business Plan
The Straightforward C.V.
Successful Public Speaking
Handling Bereavement
Play the Game-A Compendium of Rules
Individual and Personal Finance
Understanding Mental Illness
The Two Minute Message
Guide to Self Defence
Buying and Selling on Auction Sites
Buying and Selling a Property at Auction

Go to:

www.straightforwardco.co.uk